Samuel Palmer and His Etchings

The Sleeping Shepherd. Tempera and oil on wood. 15 × 20½ inches

SAMUEL PALMER

and his etchings

by

RAYMOND LISTER

FABER AND FABER
London

First published in 1969
by Faber and Faber Limited
24 Russell Square London WC1
Printed in Great Britain by
R. MacLehose & Co. Ltd
University Press Glasgow
All rights reserved

SBN 571 08978 X

To

SIR GEOFFREY KEYNES

Acknowledgements

I am grateful to everybody who has helped me in my researches for this book. I am especially grateful to Mrs. Donalda F. Palmer who has given me permission to quote hitherto unpublished extracts from Samuel Palmer's correspondence, and from A. H. Palmer's *The Life and Letters of Samuel Palmer*. I am grateful, too, to Miss Joan Linnell Ivimy for allowing me to examine letters and papers in her possession; to the Victoria and Albert Museum for permission to quote passages from the *Catalogue of an Exhibition of Drawings, Etchings & Woodcuts by Samuel Palmer and other Disciples of William Blake*; to Mr. M. B. Yeats and Macmillan and Co. Ltd. for permission to quote from the poetry of W. B. Yeats.

My thanks are due to Sir Geoffrey Keynes, Mr. Reginald Williams of the British Museum Department of Prints and Drawings, Mr. E. Chamberlain of the Fitzwilliam Museum, Mr. Hugh Macandrew of the Ashmolean Museum, Mr. Edward Malins, Mr. Basil Taylor of the Paul Mellon Foundation for British Art, Mr. Franklin White of the Samuel Palmer School of Fine Art, Shoreham, Mr. David Gould, and Mr. A. H. Driver of P. and D. Colnaghi and Co. Ltd.

My friend Mr. A. K. Astbury has made many valuable suggestions, and I am grateful to him for reading my manuscript. Finally, I should like to thank my wife Pamela for much patient help and encouragement.

R. L.
Linton 1967

[9]

Contents

Illustrations

Unless otherwise stated, the works illustrated
are by Samuel Palmer

[13]

Introduction

The paintings and drawings made by Samuel Palmer during his youth at Shoreham in Kent are among the great artistic 'discoveries' of the twentieth century. These visionary studies are portrayals of English landscape seen with an intensity of poetic and religious insight that comes most easily to an artist like Palmer in youth or adolescence. They are 'hymns sung among the hills of Paradise at eventide', as he once wrote in a pocket-book.[1] These works are the greatest things Palmer ever produced. Much of the work he produced thereafter, particularly in his middle years, was by comparison conventional, tame and unimaginative. It was not poor work – Palmer was incapable of that – but it lacked the spontaneous insight of his youthful work.

This view of Palmer's work is the one usually given by present-day commentators. So far as it goes it is accurate, but it ignores the fact that Palmer recaptured much of his lost vision in his etchings. These were made during the period from the year 1850, when he was forty-five years old, until 1881, the year of his death. There are thirteen of them, and in addition there are four others that were left unfinished when he died and which were completed by his son.

A more than usually accurate view of Palmer's work was expressed in a letter written in the 1920s by Gordon Bottomley the poet and dramatist: '[His middle years] were lost, perhaps, to his œuvre; but I ought to have seen, in the light of his long, later years of retirement, and his ability to return then to his early impulses and passions, that all his experiences had been fruitful and had worked in him to one beautiful end – and particularly in the etched work that centred about his readings in Virgil and Milton.'[2]

Such, in brief, is the theme of this book. The early visionary work remains the most important section of Palmer's œuvre; his vision was largely lost or dissipated during his middle years; it returned in the etchings made during his later life. It was less concentrated than it had been in his youth, because age generally lacks youth's enthusiasm and intensity. Palmer's early work resulted from overwhelming first-hand visionary experience. His etchings provided a quieter view of the same experiences – what Wordsworth would have described as 'emotion recollected in tranquillity',[3] even if, as we shall see, Palmer's later life was itself not tranquil.

[1] Palmer, A. H., *The Life and Letters of Samuel Palmer, Painter and Etcher* (London, 1892) p. 13.

[2] Alexander, R. G., *A Catalogue of the Etchings of Samuel Palmer* (London, 1937) p. 15. Quoted by permission of Professor Claude Colleer Abbott.

[3] 'I have said that Poetry is the spontaneous overflow of powerful feelings: it takes its origin from emotion recollected in tranquillity . . .' from Preface to *Lyrical Ballads*: edited by R. L. Brett and A. R. Jones (London 1963) p. 260.

I

The Valley of Vision

Samuel Palmer was born about 5 o'clock in the morning of 27 January 1805, at Surrey Square in the district of St. Mary in the parish of Newington, Southwark. He was the son of a Baptist bookseller, also named Samuel. The Palmer family was descended from armigerous country clergymen and, to go farther back, could claim kinship with William Wake, Archbishop of Canterbury from 1716 until his death in 1737, Sir Stephen Fox, the eighteenth-century statesman,[1] and Richard Hooker the sixteenth-century theologian. Now, however, the Palmers, with the exception of Samuel Palmer Senior, were in business as prosperous hatters, corn-factors and druggists in the City of London.

On 25 October 1803, Samuel Palmer Senior married Martha Giles at the church of St. Mary, Newington. She was the daughter of William Giles, a well-to-do banker of Walworth. The Giles were Baptists and after his marriage Palmer became one also. Giles was an amateur author, and Martha was the model for a drawing by Thomas Stothard which was engraved for the frontispiece of one of his books, *The Refuge*.[2] Giles also wrote a book *A Guide to Domestic Happiness*. 'But', wrote his great grandson A. H. Palmer, 'as I have always understood, he was a domestic martinet of the first water . . . he was the pride of his family, who meekly obeyed his orders, and worshipped him (at a very respectful distance) under the title of "The Author".'[3]

When the Palmers' first child, Samuel, was born in 1805 he was considered delicate, and was fed on 'Pap and other baby diet'.[4] But a nurse, Mary Ward, was engaged and being a young woman with no nonsense in her make-up, she at once put him on 'more substantial and unusual nutriment',[5] upon which the child began to gather strength. Miss Ward later also laid in the child's mind a foundation for a lifelong love of poetry. 'I remember', he wrote, 'the priceless value of a faithful and intelligent domestic, my nurse ; who, with little education else, was ripe in that, without which so much is often useless and mischievous — deeply read in her Bible and *Paradise Lost*. A Tonson's *Milton*, which I cherish to this day, was her present.

---

[1] For the genealogy of the Palmer family see *Stemmata Chicheleana* . . . derived from Thomas Chichele (Oxford, 1765) and *A Supplement to the Stemmata Chicheleana* (Oxford, 1775).

[2] Grigson, Geoffrey, *Samuel Palmer the Visionary Years* (London, 1947) p. 1.   [3] *Life and Letters*, p. 3.

[4] *ibid*. p. 4.   [5] *ibid*.

When less than four years old, as I was standing with her, watching the shadows on the wall from branches of elm behind which the moon had risen, she transferred and fixed the fleeting image in my memory, by repeating the couplet, –

"Vain man, the vision of a moment made,
Dream of a dream and shadow of a shade."

'I never forgot those shadows, and am often trying to paint them.'[1]

Young Samuel Palmer's life seems to have been happy. For some years he was not sent to school. His father himself undertook his education, labouring to improve the boy's 'soul and MIND . . . sitting in the house and walking in the fields'.[2] Most days, with other lessons, these words were repeated: 'Custom is the plague of wise men, and the idol of fools.'[3] Commenting on this, A. H. Palmer remarked that it was 'a rather subversive maxim for the nursery, but one for the learning of which (as I have often heard him say) my father had cause to be thankful all the days of his life. When a son of his own was beginning his career he gave him this very similar advice, "If we once lose sight of goodness as the principal thing we are adrift without an anchor. *If we merely ask ourselves 'What will people say of us?' we are rotten at the core.*" '[4]

For a time, after the birth of his younger brother, William, Samuel was sent to Merchant Taylors' School. By this time (May 1817) the Palmers had moved to Houndsditch and Merchant Taylors' School was then situated in nearby Suffolk Lane, south of Cannon Street. School did not suit Samuel and he left some time between October 1817 and March 1818.

The boy's parents thought they had discovered that he had artistic tendencies, for he had developed a passion 'for the traditions and monuments of the Church; its cloistered abbeys, cathedrals, and minsters, which I was always imagining and trying to draw; spoiling much paper with pencils, crayons, and water-colours'.[5] Artistically it was a false start, but the passion contained the seeds of a religious change, for not long after this Palmer became a member of the Church of England, and remained one for the rest of his life.

What his parents thought they had discerned as artistic tendencies were fostered and before long Samuel was applying himself to the study of art. But he had no teacher and his studies were haphazard, consisting largely of copying prints and

---

[1] *The Portfolio* No. 35, November 1872. The quotation is incorrectly given. It comes from Young's Paraphrase of Job *xxxviii*, 1. 187 and reads:

Fond man! the vision of a moment made!
Dream of a dream! and shadow of a shade!

[2] *Life and Letters*, p. 88.
[3] *Life and Letters*, pp. 5, 343. The proverb comes from Fuller, Thomas, *Gnomologia* (1732).
[4] *ibid.* p. 5.　　　　　　　　　　　　[5] *Life and Letters*, pp. 5–6.

drawings rather than of acquiring the fundamentals of drawing from models. Even such studies as he pursued were interrupted, when he was approaching the age of thirteen, by the death of his mother, an event which affected him for many years. He was a prey to melancholia throughout his life and this bereavement may have marked its onset. 'His capability of suffering', wrote his son, 'in this and other calamities cannot be gauged by his age, or by the usual standard of susceptibility, but only by his own abnormally sensitive temperament.'[1]

Soon after this Palmer was sent as a pupil to the minor artist, William Wate, who lived in George Street, off Blackfriars Lane,[2] and who exhibited from time to time at the Royal Academy and the British Institution. By the time he was fourteen, Palmer, too, was showing work in those exhibitions, and soon after his fourteenth birthday in 1819 he received the news that one of his exhibited pictures was sold. It had been bought for seven guineas by a Mr. Wilkinson of 4, Beaumont Street, Marylebone.[3]

In the same year Palmer paid his first visit to the Academy and was deeply impressed by a picture exhibited by J. M. W. Turner, his *Orange Merchantman on the Bar* (now in the Tate Gallery). From this time dated Palmer's lifelong admiration of Turner. Writing on 2 December 1872 he still remembered this picture and its original impact on him: 'The first exhibition I saw (in 1819) is fixed in my memory by the first Turner, *The Orange Merchantman on the Bar*; and, being by nature a lover of smudginess, I have revelled in him from that day to this. May not half the Art be learned from the gradations in coffee-grounds?...'[4]

Palmer again exhibited at the Academy in 1820. By this year the Palmers had moved and were living at 10 Broad Street, Bloomsbury. By this time, too, Palmer had got to know two of the young men who were later to be members of a group of disciples that gathered around the poet and artist William Blake in the closing years of his life. These were Henry Walter, Palmer's senior by six years, and Francis Oliver Finch, his senior by three years. Walter was a painter of landscape and animals, Finch a minor water-colourist who painted some charming imaginative landscapes showing the influence of his master, John Varley.

In the next year or two Palmer's pictures continued to be accepted by the Academy and the British Institution. Yet these pictures showed little originality, being reflections of the work of Turner and David Cox (whose *Treatise on Water-colour Painting* was a major influence on Palmer) and of the tame, conventional manner of his teacher, Wate. Like many young men Palmer was full of high flown theories on which he dissipated time that would have been better spent in the

---

[1] *Life and Letters*, p. 6. [2] Grigson, *op. cit.* p. 5. [3] *Life and Letters*, p. 7.
[4] *Life and Letters*, p. 343. Palmer once met Turner. 'He would speak sometimes of one well remembered occasion when, a guest at Mr. Ruskin's table, he sat next to the immortal Turner himself, and conversed with him for more than an hour' – Palmer, A. H., *Samuel Palmer A Memoir* (London, 1882) p. 14.

practice of his art. 'He was,' wrote his son, 'full of theories and speculations more suitable to the most learned professors; and full also of boyish certainty about things of which he knew very little. As far as art was concerned he continued to misuse his days, but at the same time, be it remembered, to exercise very diligently his mental faculties, till he became acquainted with Mr. John Linnell, who was his senior by twelve years, and in full career as a well-known artist.'[1] Or, to quote Palmer's own more poetic words, 'it pleased God to send Mr. Linnell as a good angel from Heaven to pluck me from the pit of modern art.'[2] This meeting took place about September 1822.[3]

Linnell was born in Bloomsbury in 1792, the son of a picture dealer and wood-carver. He showed early promise as an artist, making pencil portraits when he was ten years old. He entered the schools of the Royal Academy in 1805 and at about the same time studied under John Varley. In 1807 he received a medal for life drawing and exhibited his first work at the Academy. In the following year he exhibited at both the Academy and the British Institution. From this time onwards his work was seen in many of the important London exhibitions. He exhibited for sixty years at the Royal Academy, during which period he contributed about a hundred and seventy works. He exhibited about eighty-two works at the British Institution between 1808 and 1859.[4]

In 1818 Linnell was introduced to William Blake by George Cumberland of Bristol, who had known Blake since about 1780. Their friendship proved fruitful. To Blake, Linnell brought introductions to artists like Sir Thomas Lawrence, whom he had not previously met. He also commissioned work from Blake which included his masterpiece, *Illustrations to the Book of Job*. In return Blake was able to help Linnell in his own technique as an engraver.

Linnell was a good artist, though until about 1847 he sometimes neglected the truly imaginative side of his work – landscape – to concentrate on more remunerative portraiture. Yet he produced some delightful and imaginative studies of scenery, especially of the Surrey hills, much of it showing pastoral and harvesting subjects.

When he died in 1882, his ninetieth year, Linnell was a rich man. Yet he died without academical honours. This was partly his own fault, for he was offered membership of the Academy late in life and declined it, though he had over a period, from 1821 to 1841, applied for it several times.[5] His main reason for now refusing it appears to have been his disagreement with the electoral methods adopted by the Academy.[6]

[1] *Life and Letters*, p. 8. [2] *ibid.* p. 14.

[3] Victoria and Albert Museum *Catalogue of an Exhibition of Drawings, Etchings & Woodcuts by Samuel Palmer and other Disciples of William Blake* (London, 1926) p. 2.

[4] Story, Alfred T., *The Life of John Linnell* (London, 1892) Vol. II, p. 233.

[5] Story, *op. cit.* Vol. II, p. 164. [6] *ibid.* pp. 172–86.

John Linnell took it upon himself to advise the young Palmer in the background and practice of his art. He advised him to study especially Albert Dürer, Lucas van Leyden, Giulio Bonasone and Michelangelo, and to study human anatomy and antique sculpture. But the most significant single event of their early relationship was Linnell's introduction of Palmer to Blake. This took place on 9 October 1824 and was described by Palmer in these words :

Mr. Linnell called and went with me to Mr. Blake. We found him lame in bed, of a scalded foot (or leg). There, not inactive, though sixty-seven years old, but hard-working on a bed covered with books sat he up like one of the Antique patriarchs, or a dying Michaelangelo. Thus and there was he making in the leaves of a great book (folio) the sublimest designs from his (not superior) Dante. He said he began them with fear and trembling. I said 'O! I have enough of fear and trembling.' 'Then,' said he, 'you'll do.' He designed them (100 I think) during a fortnight's illness in bed! And there, first, with fearfulness (which had been the more, but that his designs from Dante had wound me up to forget myself), did I show him some of my first essays in design ; and the sweet encouragement he gave me (for Christ blessed little children) did not tend basely to presumption and idleness, but made me work harder and better that afternoon and night. And, after visiting him, the scene recurs to me afterwards in a kind of vision ; and in this most false, corrupt, and genteely stupid town my spirit sees his dwelling (the chariot of the sun), as it were an island in the midst of the sea — such a place is it for primitive grandeur, whether in the persons of Mr. and Mrs. Blake, or in the things hanging on the walls.[1]

This note of Palmer's may serve to remind us that he was a great maker of notes, and filled more than twenty large pocket-books with memoranda.[2] Palmer's son claimed to have destroyed them in a fire that lasted for days, with the exception of one dating from 1824 to 1825 that was owned by Palmer's friend George Richmond.[3] A. H. Palmer quoted from them extensively in his *Life and Letters of Samuel Palmer* published in 1892, but said he had done so reluctantly. 'They were never intended to be seen,' he wrote, 'and . . . they show a mental condition which, in many respects, is uninviting. It is a condition full of danger, and neither suffi-ciently masculine nor sufficiently reticent. It is, however, not without hope, and everything depends on the actions which next follow — on the strength of character available to bolt the flour from the bran.'[4]

[1] *Life and Letters*, pp. 9–10.   [2] *Life and Letters*, p. 12.
[3] Grigson, *op. cit.* p. 142 n. 7. It is now known that a second, earlier sketchbook has survived. It was recently acquired by The British Museum from a member of the Palmer family. Dating from 1819, it is smaller and slighter than the 1824 Sketchbook; it contains landscapes and sky studies.
[4] *Life and Letters*, p. 18.

Much of the memoranda indicates a highly-strung personality. Palmer's attitude to his art was certainly ecstatic :

January 2nd [1825]. – Now is begun a new year. Here I pause to look back on the time between this and about the 15th of last July. Then I laid by the [*Holy*] *Family* in much distress, anxiety, and fear ; which had plunged me into despair but for God's mercy, through which and which alone it was that despondency not for one moment slackened my sinews ; but rather, distress (being blessed) was to me a great arousement ; quickly goading me to deep humbleness, eager, restless inquiry, and diligent work. I then sought Christ's help, the giver of all good talents whether acknowledged or not, and had I gone on to seek Him as I ought, I had found His name to me as a civet-box and sweeter than all perfume. Notwithstanding, as it was, I think (by Him alone) I improved more since I resolved to depend on Him till now, than in the same time ever before ; and have felt much more assistance and consolation. For very soon after my deep humblement and distress, I resumed and finished my *Twilight*, and quickly took up my *Joseph's Dream*, and sketched in my new sketch-book. Mr. L. [Linnell] called, and looking at my *Joseph*, sepias, and sketch-books, did give me indeed sweet encouragement. Soon, by his desire, I went with him to Mr. B. [Blake], who also, on seeing my things, gave me above my hope, over-much praise ; and these praises from equally valued judgements did (God overruling) not in the least tend to presumption and idleness, and but little to pride ; for knowing my own stupidness (but not alas, to its full) I gave back the praise to God who kindly sent it and, had granted to me desponding, that at even-tide it should be light. . . .[1]

Palmer's memoranda are not all on this semi-mystical level, for more practical aspects of his art are noted here and there : 'Look for Van Leydenish qualities in real landscape, and look hard, long and continually. Look for picturesque combinations of buildings, and elegant spires and turrets for backgrounds.'[2] 'Cox is pretty – is sweet, but not grand, not profound. Carefully avoid getting into that style which is elegant and beautiful but too light and superficial ; not learned enough – like Barret. . . . Let me remember always, and may I not slumber in the possession of it, Mr. Linnell's injunction (delightful in the performance), "*Look at Albert Dürer*". . . . Look at Mr. Blake's way of relieving objects, and at his colour.'[3]

But the greatest influence on the young Palmer was the series of small wood engravings made by Blake in 1821 to illustrate the 'imitation' of Virgil's first eclogue by Ambrose Philips, in *The Pastorals of Virgil, with a course of English Reading adapted for Schools*, edited by Dr. Robert John Thornton (Plates 29 and 30). Some months after making the memoranda from which the foregoing

[1] *Life and Letters*, p. 13.   [2] *ibid*. p. 14.   [3] *ibid*. p. 15.

examples are taken, Palmer made an entry in one of his pocket books in which he praised Michelangelo and various German and Italian masters, and continued with this note on Blake's wood engravings :

I sat down with Mr. Blake's Thornton's *Virgil* woodcuts before me, thinking to give to their merits my feeble testimony. I happened first to think of their sentiment. They are visions of little dells, and nooks, and corners of Paradise ; models of the exquisitest pitch of intense poetry. I thought of their light and shade, and looking upon them I found no word to describe it. Intense depth, solemnity, and vivid brilliancy only coldly and partially describe them. There is in all such a mystic and dreamy glimmer as penetrates and kindles the inmost soul, and gives complete and unreserved delight, unlike the gaudy daylight of this world. They are like all that wonderful artist's works the drawing aside of the fleshly curtain, and the glimpse which all the most holy, studious saints and sages have enjoyed, of that rest which remaineth to the people of God. The figures of Mr. Blake have that intense, soul-evidencing attitude and action, and that elastic, nervous spring which belongs to uncaged immortal spirits. . . . Excess is the essential vivifying spirit, vital spark, embalming spice . . . of the finest art. Be ever saying to yourself 'Labour after the excess of excellence'.[1]

Blake's engravings did not please Dr. Thornton, and he ordered them to be re-engraved by a journeyman engraver. Fortunately only three of them were so treated and the remainder were saved by the urgent appeal of Linnell and other artists, probably Sir Thomas Lawrence and James Ward. Thornton agreed after all to use them, but his opinion remained unchanged, as the apologetic note he inserted in the book testifies : 'The Illustrations of this English Pastoral are by the famous BLAKE, the illustrator of *Young's* Night Thoughts, and *Blair's* Grave ; who designed and engraved them himself. This is mentioned, as they display less of art than genius, and are much admired by some eminent painters.'[2]

Some of the spirit of the Virgil wood engravings is to be discerned in many of the drawings in Palmer's 1824–5 Sketchbook.[3] Here may be seen many more of those 'little dells, and nooks, and corners of Paradise' noted by Palmer in Blake's work. There are patriarchal groups, pastoral scenes, Gothic fantasies, many of them dominated by the horned moon and evening star, symbols of Blake's

---

[1] *Life and Letters*, pp. 15–16.

[2] The best reproductions of the engravings and the best account of their creation appear in *The Illustrations of William Blake for Thornton's Virgil with The First Eclogue and the Imitation by Ambrose Philips.* Introduction by Geoffrey Keynes (London, 1937).

[3] Reproduced in 1962 by the William Blake Trust, with an introduction by Martin Butlin and a preface by Geoffrey Keynes. The original is now in the British Museum.

> ... mild & pleasant rest
> Nam'd Beulah, a soft Moony Universe, feminine, lovely,
> Pure, mild & Gentle. . . .[1]

To Blake, and to a lesser extent to his followers, the state of Beulah symbolised the state of pastoral and spiritual blessedness, sexual love, integration, a blessedness of mind only just below the highest spiritual state of all – Eden.[2] The land of Beulah is first mentioned in the Book of Isaiah:[3] 'Thou shalt no more be termed Forsaken; neither shall thy land any more be termed Desolate: but thou shalt be called Hephzi-bah, and thy land Beulah: for the Lord delighteth in thee, and thy land shall be married.' Such is the spirit to be discerned for the next few years in Palmer's paintings and in many of the works of his close friends.

These friends had begun to gather with Palmer around Blake in 1824. Francis Oliver Finch and Henry Walter have already been mentioned. Another early member of the circle was Palmer's cousin John Giles, a stockbroker, and it was he who gave the circle its name – 'The Ancients' – for he was always claiming that the ancients were superior to modern man.[4] There were, too, Welby Sherman, a draughtsman engraver; Arthur and Frederick Tatham, two brothers – Arthur was an undergraduate at Cambridge and Frederick, the elder brother, was a sculptor and miniaturist; George Richmond, the youngest member of the group, later to become a fashionable portrait painter; Edward Calvert, the oldest member of the group, who was one of the finest engravers in the history of English art. Calvert had been a midshipman in the Navy and was introduced to the group by Giles, to whom he had gone to arrange the sale of some shares.[5] Linnell was a kind of honorary 'Ancient'. That he was accepted as such is proved by a letter written to him by Palmer in September 1824, from Shoreham in Kent, which he ends by sending his best respects to Mrs. Linnell and his love to the 'little Ancients' – the deduction from this being that the 'little Ancients' were children of an adult 'Ancient' – Linnell.[6]

Palmer stated in a letter printed in *The Portfolio*, that he was forced into the country by illness (thought to have been bronchitis coupled with asthma)[7] and remained there with his father for about seven years. 'There, sometimes by ourselves, sometimes visited by friends of congenial taste, literature, and art and

---

[1] *The Four Zoas* I. 94–6.

[2] For a fuller explanation of the meaning of Blake's states see Lister, Raymond, *William Blake. An Introduction to the Man and to his Work* (London, 1968).

[3] Chapter 62, Verse iv.

[4] [Calvert, Samuel], *A Memoir of Edward Calvert Artist by his Third Son* (London, 1893) p. 62.

[5] Lister, Raymond, *Edward Calvert* (London, 1962) p. 11.

[6] Ivimy MSS. Another letter, dated 21 December 1828, has a similar ending: *Life and Letters*, pp. 173–7.

[7] *ibid.* p. 49.

[24]

ancient music wiled away the hours, and a small independence made me heedless, for the time of further gain.'[1] This was at Shoreham, and the letter written in 1824 to Linnell from which I have quoted in the previous paragraph, proves that Palmer was there somewhat earlier than had previously been known.[2] The move to Shoreham was made possible by a legacy amounting probably to £3,000 from his grandfather Giles, 'The Author', who died in 1825.[3]

Shoreham was (and still is) a beautiful place. Of the valley in which it is set Calvert said, 'It looked as if the Devil had not yet found it out!'[4]

London (wrote A. H. Palmer) is only twenty miles away; but years ago, a distance now disposed of by a few puffs of steam kept back that foul tide that has crept little by little over so much of Kent and Surrey. No unsavoury crowds defiled the sweet air with their ribaldry, and no shrieking engine startled the hares from their twilight supper, or the herons from their patient watch over the shallows. Everything connected with the little village in those happy times seemed wrapped about with a sentiment of cosy, quiet antiquity, full of associations that carried you far back into the pastoral life of merry England, years ago.

Lingering on in the ancestral parks stood many a 'shattered veteran' of a thousand winters' gales, glad enough at last to rest his aged limbs upon the ground they had shaded for centuries . . .

Spring clothed the innumerable orchards with clotted blossom, and Autumn never failed to fulfil this fair promise by lavishing the fruits in such profusion that the very leaves seemed in hiding, and the boughs were bent lower and lower till their treasure rested on the grass. Rich too were the harvests that the kindly soil gave to her sunburnt children, whose dress was beautiful and whose every implement was archaic. No grudging machinery clawed away the gleaner's perquisite, but they toiled on till the harvest-moon gilded their faces and the hungry owl gave them shrill warning of his supper-time . . .

The moon herself bore little resemblance to the pallid, small reality we see above us nowadays. She seemed to blush and bend herself towards men (as when she stooped to kiss Endymion in olden time) casting a warm, romantic glow over the landscape that slept at her feet.[5]

Here it was that the 'Ancients' foregathered, meeting at Palmer's cottage[6] (nicknamed 'Rat Abbey') and at Water House, his father's house, living simply,

---

[1] *The Portfolio, loc. cit.*   [2] Grigson, *op. cit.* p. 30.   [3] Grigson, *op. cit.* p. 49.
[4] Calvert, *Memoir*, p. 33.   [5] *Life and Letters*, pp. 39–41.
[6] It is not known if Palmer actually lived in this cottage. He owned five cottages; they still exist, but it is not possible to ascertain which one was 'Rat Abbey'. They were surveyed and valued in 1835. Water House also still exists. Despite a somewhat pretentious appearance it is quite small, especially considering that it was occupied by another man – Benjamin Russell – as well as by the Palmers. Communicated by Mr. C. Franklin White.

eating apples and bread, drinking green tea, and bathing in the Darent. They painted, recited poetry aloud, watched the heavens by night, investigated reported hauntings and enacted romantic scenes. F. O. Finch's widow later described these entertainments:

But the favourite haunt was a wild lane near Shoreham in Kent, flanked on each side with great old beech trees; it was hedged in by their spreading roots in the wildest contortions, until a disciple of 'Progress' having been made surveyor of the roads shaved them smooth with the most liberal use of the hatchet. Some years before it had been the scene of a murder, and while in its pristine wildness and grandeur it was most admirably adapted as the theatre for the enactment of some of the scenes of witchcraft so popular among the Tableaux vivans [*sic*]. They all knew the Macbeth music by heart, and many a night made the 'black lane' ring with it. The country people called them 'extologers' [*sic*], and believed their camp stools to be magical instruments. They were always to be seen abroad in thunderstorms. These were their freaks but their usual talk was of high and solemn things – their 'chamber of horrors' being only a kind of intellectual 'smoking-room'.[1]

The word 'extollagers', wrote Laurence Binyon, 'suggests somehow the mood of abstracted exaltation in which the young artists passed their nights and days'.[2] According to John Lewis Roget the word is probably a corruption of astrologer. 'Samuel Palmer,' he wrote, 'in a letter to Mr. Jenkins, explains "extollager" as one who "went by the stars, a strange gentleman whose sketching stool, unseen before in those parts, was mistaken for a celestial instrument"'.[3]

They sang songs in cornfields under the harvest moon. Sometimes Palmer played on a violin.[4] They read to one another out of old Palmer's books, especial favourites being the Gothic novels of Ann Radcliffe;[5] the poetry of Shakespeare, Milton and Keats; John Fletcher's *The Faithful Shepherdess* and John Flavel's *Husbandry Spiritualized*. Palmer loved poetry and wrote some himself – verses like these taken from the 1824–5 Sketchbook:[6]

[1] Finch, Mrs. Eliza, *Memorials of the late Francis Oliver . . . with Selections from his Writings* (London, 1865) pp. 45–6.

[2] Binyon, Laurence, *The Followers of William Blake* (London, 1925) p. 15.

[3] *A History of the 'Old Water-Colour' Society* (London, 1891) Vol. I, p. 520.

[4] Palmer, *A Memoir*, pp. 14, 28. F. O. Finch was a good singer. See Finch, *Memorials*, pp. 330–51: 'Of the late Francis Finch, as a Musician, by his old friend, Alfred Roffe.'

[5] Palmer's copy of Ann Radcliffe's *The Mysteries of Udolpho* (2nd ed., 1794) is in the library of Sir Geoffrey Keynes.

[6] The poem is printed in full in *Garland* edited by F. Warner (Cambridge, 1968). The section above is reprinted by permission of the Trustees of the British Museum.

And now the trembling light
Glimmers behind the little hills, and corn,
Lingring as loth to part : yet part thou must
And though than open day far pleasing more
(Ere yet the fields and pearled cups of flowers
    Twinkle in the parting light ;)
Thee night shall hide, sweet visionary gleam
That softly lookest through the rising dew :
    Till all like silver bright ;
    The Faithful Witness, pure, and white,
Shall look o'er yonder grassy hill,
At this village, safe, and still.
All is safe, and all is still,
Save what noise the watch-dog makes
Or the shrill cock the silence breaks
    – Now and then. –
    And now and then –
    Hark ! – once again,
    The wether's bell
    To us doth tell
Some little stirring in the fold.

Years later, in 1872, he wrote in a letter of the inspiring qualities of old poetry in connexion with his etchings. 'O ! the joy – colours and brushes pitched out of the window ; plates the *Liber Studiorum* size got out of the dear, little etching-cupboard where they have long reposed ; great needles sharpened three-corner-wise like bayonets ; opodeldoc rubbed into the forehead to wake the brain up ; and a Great Gorge of old poetry to get up the dreaming ; for, after all, *that's* "the seasoning as does it".'[1]

But the 'Ancients' were not all earnestness, and a good sense of fun pervaded the circle. To quote Mrs. Finch again :

. . . There was no lack of the comic element among them – for they would condescend at times to things of earth with all the oddities found there which they treated in their own peculiar racy fashion – so varied was their humour ; and often have the still woods been heard to ring with their joyous laughter.

The appearance the group presented was somewhat motley, the eschewing the things of fashion being one of the great principles which they did not fail to carry out in practice. One of the party [Palmer] was particularly remarkable from a certain

[1] *Life and Letters*, p. 338.

baldness on the forehead which, added to a flowing beard, (a thing to be looked at in those days) together with a cloak down almost to the heels, gave him to passers by the appearance of an apparition, by no means an unpleasant one, but certainly not youthful. On one occasion they entered Bromley churchyard, in which of course they delighted to linger – gazing with fond reverence on its dim grey tower ere it stole forth in the summer dawn and at the ancient monuments so quiet and so solemn, as to banish all thoughts save those of harmony and peace – but un-fortunately this was about the time of the 'body snatching' and an old man, who was boxed up as a sentry, had perceived one or two of the foremost enter, and had noted their coats too, carried knapsack-wise, which looked very much to his suspicious and peering eyes as sacks rolled up. So the friends after a leisurely survey of the old church, on turning the corner of the tower which had partially hidden them, were encountered by a gruff voice and a bayonet fastened on what appeared to them, the handle of a broom-stick. The victim at whom the bayonet was pointed and who was the foremost of the group, merely said, 'This is a fine old church of yours', and the coolness of the remark, together with the appearance of three or four fresh heads seen behind that of the speaker, so startled and con-fused the 'ancient guardian', that he could only stammer out, 'Yes, very! good-night, gentlemen', and immediately disappeared! The pilgrims continuing their way, came near Beckingham[1] Church while it was yet dawn, and observing a sort of well in a recess by the way side were minded to wash off some of the dust of their journey. In utter silence they pulled off their coats and waistcoats, threw them down anywhere, bent Narcissus like over the fountain, and were just about to enjoy a delightful wash – when suddenly, at that strange hour, was heard the tramp of footsteps, and a number of men, cricketers, returning late from a carouse, observing some movement in the recess of the well side, hemmed in the washers; each of whom in the scuffle that preceded, clutched at the coat and waistcoat nearest, whether his own or not – and the countrymen, after some discussion, decided that this must be a party of runaway school-boys, and that it would be well to march them into the village, awake the constable, and put them into the cage until the morning. But at this moment the venerable scalp of the friend we have mentioned, saved the whole party; for a half tipsy little man, coming up to him, ran his finger against the grain of the sparely bristled forehead, exclaiming. 'What on earth have we here? Oh no, these ain't school-boys, this is an old file!' upon which the cricketers with a burst of uproarious laughter went their way; and on passing the village cage, it appeared that the pilgrims would not have enjoyed it all by themselves, as some of the cricketer's friends had been safely lodged there under watch and ward; and they feeling that

[1] Now Beckenham.

'Soft stillness and the night
Become the touches of sweet harmony',

were practising in full chorus — much to their own edification. One of the youths
who so narrowly escaped the cage has sat for many years on the magisterial bench,
well beneficed, and is now a reverend prebendary.[1] After another of their night
rambles, and about eight or nine in the morning, as they were passing the house of a
hospitable friend of Francis Finch's, he, feeling himself unable to continue the
march, knocked at the door; when the kind host, seeing by his jaded looks that
the fire of his enthusiasm had all burnt out, after giving him a comfortable breakfast, tucked him up in as comfortable a bed, where he slept soundly in a state of
utter unconsciousness until the evening . . .[2]

On the whole this period in the young men's lives was one of innocence, of
ecstatic awareness of the spiritual qualities inherent in the landscape, and of the
sacramental qualities in the interchange of the seasons. 'Earth spiritualised, not
Heaven naturalised', as Calvert's son wrote.[3] 'I feel,' said Calvert — and the same
could have been said by Palmer — 'a yearning to see the glades and nooks receding
like vistas into the gardens of Heaven.'[4]

All of these sentiments are well expressed in Palmer's Shoreham paintings.
We may also see in them the influence of his reading, of his taste and of his friends,
for Palmer was sensitive to outside influences. We have seen that Milton influenced him from an early age, and we shall see later that in his closing years he
made etchings inspired by Milton and illustrated his minor poems. The poem
quoted on page 27, 'And now the trembling light,' has echoes from such works
as *Il Penseroso* and *L'Allegro*. Such lines as these from *Il Penseroso* probably set
up in his mind a train of ideas that was to lead to the rich imaginings of his drawing
'Late Twilight' (Plate 18):

I walk unseen
On the dry smooth-shaven Green,
To behold the wandering Moon,
Riding neer her highest noon,
Like one that had bin led astray
Through the heav'n's wide pathles way;
And oft, as if her head she bow'd,
Stooping through a fleecy cloud.

[1] Arthur Tatham; he was Prebendary of Exeter, 1860–74.   [2] Finch, *Memorials*, pp. 46–50.
[3] Calvert, *Memoir*, p. 24.   [4] *ibid.* p. 25.

Palmer's reading also included the works of John Bunyan, James Hervey, John Clare and George Crabbe. It is not difficult to see in his Shoreham paintings of moonlight and twilight reminiscences of such lines as these from Clare's sonnet *Twilight*:

> The setting Sun withdraws his yellow light,
>   A gloomy staining shadows over all,
> While the brown beetle, trumpeter of Night,
>   Proclaims his entrance with a droning call.
> How pleasant now, where slanting hazels fall
>   Thick, o'er the woodland stile, to muse and lean;
> To pluck a woodbine from the shade withal,
>   And take short snatches o'er the moisten'd scene;
> While deep and deeper shadows intervene,
>   And leave fond Fancy moulding to her will
> The cots, and groves, and trees so dimly seen,
>   That die away more undiscerned still;
> Bringing a sooty curtain o'er the sight,
> And calmness in the bosom still as night.

In the visual arts Claude's poetic painted and etched landscapes and Bonasone's engravings profoundly affected Palmer and his fellow 'Ancients'. Calvert wrote how 'Claude and Bonasone frequently present us with forms of child-like grace and innocence seated in recesses of woodland growth — the freshness of an early age — midst seeming pathways, threading the mysteries of retreat to seclusions of blessedness, that make one laugh outright from very joyfulness of soul'.[1] Finch, too, in his water-colours was influenced by Claude, but Finch was less of a 'visionary' than either Claude or Palmer. It was Blake who pointed out to the 'Ancients' the delights of Claude. 'Among spurious old pictures', wrote Palmer in a letter to Blake's biographer, Alexander Gilchrist, 'he had met with many "Claudes", but spoke of a few which he had seen, really untouched and unscrubbed, with the greatest delight; and mentioned, as a peculiar charm, that in these, when minutely examined, there were, upon the focal lights of the foliage, small specks of pure white which made them appear to be glittering with dew which the morning sun had not yet dried up. . . . His description of these genuine Claudes, I shall never forget. He warmed with his subject, and it continued through an evening walk. The sun was set; but Blake's Claudes made sunshine in that shady place.'[2] Such glittering 'small specks of pure white' may often be seen in Palmer's paintings and etchings.

---

[1] Calvert, *Memoir*, p. 19.
[2] Gilchrist, Alexander, *Life of William Blake*, ed. Ruthven Todd (London, 1942) p. 311.

As we have seen, Linnell introduced Palmer to the engravings of Bonasone, which were to influence him not only in his Shoreham paintings, but also in his etchings. Much later in his life, on 8 July 1871, Palmer wrote a letter to Philip Gilbert Hamerton, the etcher and author of *Etching and Etchers*,[1] in which he said: 'Bonasoni is to me the great copper master of shadows: he never commits the grievous fault of making shadow, as such, rich and of a positive texture; and his lines, if not etched, as I have sometimes suspected, are more like etching than those of any other engraver.'[2] In November 1872, to the same correspondent, he wrote: 'Bonasoni seems to me the greatest master of shadowing upon copper. . . . Let any one who can draw, copy exactly in pen and ink some boldly-shadowed limb of Bonasoni's, and afterwards turn it into a tree-trunk by vigorous line work expressing the textures of the bark, and he will then see texture in its proper function, and shadow in its poetic sleep.'[3]

The imaginative painting (and later the etching) of shadow is characteristic of Palmer's work. Perhaps this suggests another of his literary influences, that of John Keats, who in his *Ode to a Nightingale*, wrote of 'embalmed darkness':

> I cannot see what flowers are at my feet,
> Nor what soft incense hangs upon the boughs,
> But, in embalmed darkness, guess each sweet.[4]

And indeed the opening line of Keats's sonnet *To Sleep* might have been addressed to Palmer: 'O soft embalmer of the still midnight'.

Other influences on Palmer's Shoreham paintings were Henry Fuseli, Alexander Cozens, Pieter Brueghel the Elder and Adam Elsheimer. The influence of his brother 'Ancients' must not be overlooked, in particular that of Calvert. Throughout his life Palmer kept some of Calvert's engravings in a portfolio; he called them 'mind toners'.[5]

In 1826 Palmer made what is, so far as is known, his only wood engraving, 'Harvest under a Waning Moon' (Plate 19).[6] It is probably this little work to which Palmer refers in a letter written to Richmond from Calvert's house on 3 January 1827: 'Would you do me the favour to give my best respects to Mr. Sherman & tell him I rather wish that my block should not be proved & retouch'd – the getting a bad proof such as they give at the shops inclining artists to retouch & Mr. Calvert says no wood engravers can with advantage retouch after prooving & that they all have regretted it when they have so done.'[7]

[1] London, 1868.   [2] *Life and Letters*, p. 315.   [3] *Life and Letters*, p. 333.
[4] This was a favourite quotation of F. O. Finch. Finch, *Memorials*, p. 44.
[5] *Life and Letters*, p. 153. The best reproductions of Calvert's engravings appear in *Edward Calvert: Eleven Engravings* (Cambridge, 1966).
[6] But cf. pp. 47, 56, 121-4, for works that he drew on the wood for others to engrave.   [7] Richmond MSS.

The remark made by Palmer's son concerning Calvert's 'Chamber Idyll' could with justice be applied to Palmer's wood engraving: 'It is doubly condensed poetry.'[1] The horned waning moon lies on its back to the right of clumps of trees, in front of which, at the other side, slopes a gentle hill. A cornfield reaches from the foreground to the distant trees, and in this, at the left, stands a tiny thatched cottage In the right foreground stand shocks of corn-sheaves, and to the left workers kneel and stoop at their work of cutting the corn with sickles and tying it into sheaves. The moon throws a light over the field, the heads of corn coruscating in it. The lower part of the sky still reflects the last faint illuminations of the vanished sun, or as Palmer himself later described it, 'the infinitely retiring eastern sky during the western after-glow'.[2]

The richness of the visionary landscapes in Palmer's Shoreham paintings is symbolised by the breast-like shapes of the hills, the little cottages with curved roofs, and the great masses of cloud, cirro-cumulus and alto-cumulus or *moutons*,[3] these latter reflecting, as it were, in the sky the flocks of sheep on the rich earth below. Fruit swells or ripens on the trees and the corn grows with great heads that might almost be bunches of grapes.

If cornfields and moonlight were common subjects in Palmer's 'visionary' works, so also were horse-chestnut trees (Plate 20). Mr. Geoffrey Grigson has pointed out that Palmer and Tennyson, who were contemporaries, were among the first to make use of horse-chestnuts in English painting and literature.[4] Until their time these beautiful trees had been largely ignored or even condemned, as by William Gilpin, who wrote, 'The whole tree together in flower is a glaring object, totally unharmonious and unpicturesque.'[5] One exception to this was John Evelyn the diarist who in his *Directions for the Gardiner at Says-Court*, written in 1687, mentions 'The *Constantinople*, or *Horse-Chessnut*', which, he says 'is beautifull for greate walks & Avenues'.[6] To Palmer 'A cedar and a chestnut are just the best trees you could be employed upon'.[7] Tennyson used the horse-chestnut in some of the brief but illuminating allusions to natural phenomena with which his work abounds, as here:

> Calm is the morn without a sound,
> Calm as to suit a calmer grief,
> And only thro' the faded leaf
> The chestnut pattering to the ground.[8]

---

[1] *Life and Letters*, p. 30.   [2] *ibid.* p. 363.

[3] Cirro-cumulus are known to the French as *petits moutons*, alto-cumulus as *gros moutons*.

[4] Grigson, *op. cit.* p. 34. See also Grigson, Geoffrey, *The Harp of Aeolus* (London, 1948) pp. 79–85.

[5] *Remarks on Forest Scenery* (2nd ed. 1794) Vo. I, p. 65.

[6] First published by the Nonesuch Press (London, 1932), edited by Geoffrey Keynes, p. 42.

[7] *Life and Letters*, p. 213.   [8] *In Memoriam*, XI.

1. The Willow
Etching. $3\frac{17}{32} \times 2\frac{5}{8}$ inches. State I

Mrs. Raymond Lister

2. The Skylark
Etching. $3\frac{7}{8} \times 2\frac{7}{8}$ inches. State V

Ashmolean Museum

3. The Herdsman's Cottage *or* Sunset
Etching. $3\frac{13}{16} \times 3$ inches. State II
Mrs. Raymond Lister

4. Christmas *or* Folding the Last Sheep
Etching. $3\frac{7}{8} \times 3\frac{3}{16}$ inches. State IV
Mrs. Raymond Lister

5. The Vine *or* Plumpy Bacchus
Etching. Upper subject : $3\frac{1}{2} \times 5$ inches. Lower subject : $2\frac{1}{4} \times 5$ inches.
State IV

Mrs. Raymond Lister

6. The Sleeping Shepherd; Early Morning
Etching. $3\frac{3}{4} \times 3\frac{1}{16}$ inches. State IV
Mrs. Raymond Lister

7. The Rising Moon *or* An English Pastoral
Etching. $4\frac{19}{32} \times 7\frac{1}{2}$ inches. State VII
Ashmolean Museum

8. The Wearly Ploughman *or* The Herdsman *or* Tardus Bubulcus
Etching. $5\frac{3}{16} \times 7\frac{15}{16}$ inches. State VIII

Mrs. Raymond Lister

9. The Early Ploughman *or* The Morning Spread upon the Mountains
Etching. $5\frac{1}{8}$ to $5\frac{3}{16} \times 7\frac{3}{4}$ inches. State VI
Ashmolean Museum

Gerard Manley Hopkins, a younger contemporary of Palmer and Tennyson, also loved the horse-chestnut and many references to it may be found in his writings, as in his poem *Pied Beauty*, in which he writes of 'Fresh-firecoal chestnut-falls'. In Henry Alexander Bowler's picture, painted in 1856, 'The Doubt: "Can these dry bones live" ', the tree is used to symbolise resurrection.[1] Indeed from this time the horse-chestnut becomes firmly established in English art and letters. In Palmer's work it was to reappear, as we shall see, in his etchings.

In the technique employed by Palmer in some of his Shoreham drawings the quality of the lines in his etchings seems to be anticipated. In these drawings he mixed sepia water-colour with gum and the lines were drawn so thickly that they stand up from the paper like etched or engraved lines. When the drawings were completed they were coated with varnish which added extra depth and richness to them. The reader may think that I exaggerate in claiming that the thick lines of Palmer's varnished drawings are like etched lines, which are in fact usually thinner. However, it is also true that some etchings have lines just as thick as those on Palmer's drawings. One such etching was probably known to Palmer; this is Edward Calvert's 'Back View of a Woman's Head Looking Down',[2] a tiny work measuring $3 \times 1\frac{3}{4}$ inches, printed on brown paper. The only impression known is in the British Museum. The richness of the lines in the Shoreham drawings adds considerably to the impression they convey of the richness of nature, and it may have been that this was one reason for Palmer's turning later to etching as a favourite medium.

In 1834 Welby Sherman made a mezzotint after a painting by Palmer – 'Evening'. It bears the inscription: 'EVENING LATE, BY THEN THE CHEWING FLOCKS/HAD TA'EN THEIR SUPPERS OF THE SAVOURY HERB/OF KNOT-GRASS DEW-BESPRENT.' It is of the richest imaginable texture and may have been yet another factor in turning Palmer to etching, for although it is a different technique it is sufficiently related to it to have suggested its possibilities.

But let us return to Palmer's relationship with Linnell. Despite the fact that Palmer had seen him as his 'good angel from Heaven', he did not agree with everything his mentor tried to tell him. Linnell was no visionary, nor did he understand the visionary's mind. Once when Calvert was showing one of his works to Miss Linnell, he said, 'These are God's fields, this is God's brook, and these are God's sheep and lambs.' Linnell, who was present, sarcastically asked him, 'Then why don't you mark them with a big G?'[3]

Linnell urged Palmer to use greater naturalism in his work. But, wrote Palmer in a letter of September 1828 to Richmond, 'I will not infringe a penny on the money God has sent me, beyond the interest, but live & study in patience & hope.

[1] Lister, Raymond, *Victorian Narrative Paintings* (London, 1966) pp. 84–5.
[2] Lister, *Calvert*, plate XV and p. 64.   [3] Story, A. T., *James Holmes and John Varley* (London, 1894) p. 105.

By God's help I will not sell away His gift of art for money; no, not for fame neither, which is far better. Mr. Linnell tells me that by making studies of the Shoreham scenery I could get a thousand a year directly. Tho' I am making studies for Mr. Linnell, I will, God help me, never be a naturalist by profession.'[81] Replying to this, Richmond wrote: 'I was delighted to hear of your inflexibility . . . for though it is certain *you will not* any more than *Mr. Blake* get a thousand a year by it yet you will have what he had a contentment in your own mind such as gold cannot purchase – or flimsy praise procure. Mr. Linnell is an extraordinary man but he is not a Mr. Blake . . .'[2]

Yet Linnell was not completely wrong. Palmer would not at that time have made an adequate living from the kind of painting he was producing. Despite the fact that his work was frequently accepted for exhibition at the Royal Academy, his income remained small. There were also signs in his paintings that his period of intense vision was ending. Moreover, he saw less of his friends and was becoming something of a recluse in his valley. Only Sherman and Walter continued to be frequent visitors to Shoreham, and although he saw Finch and Calvert at monthly meetings at which the 'Ancients' foregathered to discuss their problems and ideas and to exchange views,[3] he saw less of Richmond who was now married,[4] and of Arthur Tatham, who was now ordained. There were, too, ominous signs that the valley itself would lose its idyllic calm. The Reform Bill was about to be passed and ricks were burned around Shoreham.

Palmer had received another bequest[5] and in 1832 with part of it he bought a house in London, No. 4, Grove Street, Lisson Grove; it no longer exists. Some of the 'Ancients' – Calvert, Richmond and Linnell – lived within easy distance of Lisson Grove. Palmer did not just yet quit Shoreham completely, but returned there from time to time. With the remainder of his bequest he bought two Shoreham cottages as an investment. But his finances were shaky and the sales of his works were small. He calculated that 'the expenses of one person living as an epic poet should live could be cut down to 5s. 2d. a week; but the old memorandum books reveal that he found it no easy matter to achieve this economy. For instance the poet's estimated nightly allowance of one candle grievously curtailed the nocturnal talks and readings to which all "The Ancients" were so much addicted'.[6]

---

[1] Richmond MSS.

[2] *Victoria and Albert Museum Catalogue*, p. 9. Writing of Linnell in 1836, Crabb Robinson the diarist wrote that he had asked Palmer 'whether Linnell is not a man of worldly wisdom. He understood the insinuation and said: "Only *defensively*", and he represented Linnell's conduct as having been very generous towards Blake. This is contrary to my impression concerning Linnell. . . .' Hudson, Derek (Editor) *The Diary of Henry Crabb Robinson. An Abridgement*. Oxford University Press, London, 1967, p. 159.

[3] Lister, *Calvert*, pp. 43–4.

[4] Richmond eloped with Frederick Tatham's sister Julia, whose father had forbidden the marriage.

[5] *Life and Letters*, p. 54.   [6] *Life and Letters*, p. 54.

He was dissatisfied with his work. 'My father,' wrote A. H. Palmer, 'was also perturbed by faults which he now began to discern in his practice and style, and he catalogues them as follows. "Some of my faults. *Feebleness* of first conception through bodily weakness, and consequent timidity of execution. No first-conceived, and *shapely* effect. No rich, flat body of local colours as a ground. No first-conceived foreground, or figures.

Whites too raw.	Greens crude.
Greys cold.	Shadows purple.

RIDGES OF MOUNTAIN ALONG OPEN COUNTRY."

'This list is followed by suggestions for his future practice :

"(1) Base the subject on a neutral-tint effect like Varley's little drawing, so that at the beginning the great shapes of the lights shall be forcibly announced. (2A) Invent at once the great masses of Local Colour, and aim at once at a splendid arrangement. (B) Blocks of local colour before the small varieties. (3) Carry on the drawing till real illumination be obtained. Investigate on some simple object what are the properties of illumination and shade. (4) If possible, complete at whatever struggle the foreground and figures at the time. (5) Let everything be colour, and not sullied with blackness. Think of some of Titian's things, as *The Entombment*. (6) CLEANNESS OF TINT. Try to get something beautiful in the first design." '[1]

Palmer was in fact becoming restless. Shoreham no longer had power to move him. He looked farther afield for his inspiration and a definite direction was taken in 1834 after he had seen 'some third-rate print of Combe Martin Bay . . . in a shop-window'.[2] Thus moved, he visited Devon and in the few remaining pictures belonging to his youthful period we find Devon rocks and tors in the midst of Shoreham cornfields.

In 1835 Palmer took another journey, this time by steamer, from London to Wales. His companion was Henry Walter. By 1836 he had left Shoreham altogether and lived in Grove Street with his old nurse, Mary Ward. In that year he made another journey to Wales, this time with Calvert.

It was on one of these Welsh expeditions that Palmer first met Charles West Cope the artist, who was later to be an early influence in his etching. F. M. Redgrave recorded the meeting. 'It was during a tour in Wales that my father and Cope first made acquaintance with Samuel Palmer, the water-colour painter. They were sitting, miserably enough, round their inn fire, one sadly raining day, when they saw a figure approaching the inn door, very wet, and very strangely clothed. They first took him for a pedlar, but the pedlar turned out to be a painter;

---

[1] *Life and Letters*, pp. 54-5.　　　　　[2] *ibid.* p. 55.

his wares, pack, etc., were arrangements devised by himself for storing his whole painting apparatus, clothes, and necessaries of travel upon his own person.'[1]

The water-colours made by Palmer on these journeys are entirely different from his Shoreham work. They are more conventional, more realistic, though highly competent. They might be by a different painter. Finest among them are studies of waterfalls.[2]

Palmer's youth and vision were fast flying away, and in 1837 came an event that was to prove their vanishing point. This was the death of Miss Ward, which he recorded in these words :

Jany—18–1837 at about ¼ past 4 I asked Mary Ward to bid God bless me – & to kiss me (as I kissed her) she said 'May the Lord bless you forever & ever' & kissed me quickly several times on the cheek though so exhausted – my Brother William asked her to bless him & kiss him – & she said 'May the Lord God Almighty & Jesus Christ – here her voice failed – & she kissed him on the cheek –

My dear Nurse & most faithful servant & friend Mary Ward died at 5 minutes to five o'clock 18th Jany 1837 the same day of the same month on which my Mother died confined to bed 11 days.[3]

---

[1] *Richard Redgrave* (London, 1891) p. 51.

[2] Henry Crabb Robinson met Palmer on his 1836 journey to Wales; he recorded the event in his diary: 'Aug. 4th [*Dol y Melynllyn*]. . . . After our breakfast the yet unknown artist [Samuel Palmer], whose eye of deep feeling and very capacious forehead had inspired me with predilections for him, prepared to set out to one of the waterfalls I was come to see. I proposed to accompany him, and so an acquaintance was formed. He incidentally spoke of Blake as the greatest genius in art of modern times, though little known.' *The Diary of Henry Crabb Robinson. An Abridgement*, p. 159.

[3] *Victoria and Albert Museum Catalogue*, p. 25.

II

The Vale of Experience

Palmer had become engaged to Linnell's nineteen-year-old daughter Hannah – or Anny as he called her. From a letter which has survived, written by her to Samuel, it appears that to Hannah at any rate their courtship was an idyllic experience.

Tuesday June 14

My dear dear Mr. Palmer.

I take a few moments to write to you because I think it will please you to hear that my affection so far from decreasing in your absence increases daily. I think of you more than ever and look forward to your coming back with stronger emotions of joy than I before now felt. I feel unhappy when you are absent. I want your conversation and society which is dearer to me than any other. I want you of an evening to walk with. Yesterday evening I took a delightful walk with poor Uncle George who is ordered up here for his health, but I could not help wishing I was with you walking through those delightful places we so much enjoy. Oh a Summer evening walk with you is beyond every thing delight. I am afraid you will remember me only as a poor pale creature forlorn and miserable with all my enthusiasm and ardour worn out but I can assure you it is far otherwise. I have now recovered my health with this nice warm weather and am as lively and sprightly as ever.

I could write much more but am afraid if I stay I shall not be able to send it at the time you mention and though few are the words yet you will remember that they come with sincerity and truth from one who is yours most faithfully and affectionately for ever

Hannah Linnell

P.S. you must excuse the bad writing as no one knows of it. I have written it by stealth expecting every moment to be discovered. Do not trouble to write again nor you must not expect another from me.[1]

Some months after Miss Ward's death, on 30 September 1837, the couple were married at the Registrar's Office, Marylebone. The form of civil marriage was at Linnell's insistence, and Palmer's son comments, 'as such [it] must have given a staunch churchman like my father no little pain.'[2] Palmer himself wrote this

---

[1] Ivimy MSS.   [2] *Life and Letters*, p. 59.

comment in a commonplace-book : 'S.P. was married at the Court-house, Maryle-bone ; he, a churchman !'[1] Richmond and Calvert witnessed the ceremony.[2] Four days later the newly-weds set out with Mr. and Mrs. Richmond for a holiday in Italy.

The Italian trip was on the whole a happy period in the Palmers' lives, despite the fact that throughout it there was a constant flow of letters from Hannah's parents in which the young couple's activities were subjected to close surveillance. But that was not altogether unusual in a period during which the paterfamilias enjoyed undisputed authority. In any case the Linnells were sufficiently distant from the newly-weds to remain a comparatively abstract influence.

On their way to Italy, Samuel and Hannah were delayed in Paris by passport difficulties. But this delay afforded them an opportunity to savour some of the delights of the French capital, in particular those at the Louvre where they noticed the Titians, the Giorgiones and Veronese's great 'Marriage at Cana'. They saw, too, chestnut trees, lakes and fountains in the Tuileries gardens. They saw three weddings and other services, all celebrated in 'a Gothic Church much finer than Notre Dame'. And they savoured French cooking – four courses, fruit, wine and brandy for the equivalent of one shilling and eightpence a head.[3]

They continued their journey to Rome, passing through picturesque and romantic Alpine scenery, noticing 'archaic tumbrels full of grapes drawn by cream-coloured oxen with "faces like poets", and guided by ideally picturesque peasants'.[4] They passed through Milan where they saw a procession of boys carrying a corpse on a bier. The boys were dressed in white and wore pasteboard wings which knocked against everything they passed, making an uncelestial clatter. They saw, too, Leonardo's 'Last Supper' in Santa Maria delle Grazie. Farther on, in Florence, they saw works by Michelangelo, Andrea del Sarto and other masters. There they also met an English artist who visited the Opera every evening to keep warm, as he had found this was cheaper than burning a fire. But Rome itself with its art treasures, ruins, fountains, monks, oxen, papal processions, carnivals, and above all its brilliant sunshine, surpassed everything else that they had seen.

Palmer himself described many of these sights and experiences, in Rome and elsewhere, in a letter written from Pozzuoli a year later, on 28 October 1838, to his cousin, Samuel Giles.

An account of all the novelties which I have seen, if hung from the top of the Monument, would trail upon London Bridge ; therefore I will just mention a few things as they occur to me, and waive all introductories excepting an apology for

---

[1] *Life and Letters*, p. 59.　　　　[2] Story, A. T., *Life of John Linnell* (London, 1892) Vol. I. p. 199.
[3] Letter from the Palmers to the Linnells, October 1837. Ivimy MSS.
[4] *Life and Letters*, p. 60.

having seemed to neglect you so long, occasioned by a continual press of labour and study, which has prevented my writing a line to any one, but in our periodical letters to Bayswater.[1] Yet, many a time, have I sat down in spirit by your cheerful and intellectual fireside, where have passed some of my very happiest hours.

The inside of a Romish church was the first novelty which presented itself; not a believer's band-box, in which the greatest quantity of lace caps and laces are crowded into the smallest possible space, partitioned out into dress boxes called pews, for the comfort of consciences too tender for the opera; where fine ladies cover their heads with *Valenciennes* to play at hide and seek with the angels (by which, perhaps, were meant, says Dr. Gill, young ministers), and making what is called a *respectable* congregation — a *thriving interest*. Not this, but a refuge for the abject and the outcast, the peasant and the pilgrim; with no *free seats*, where all are free, to publish his poverty — no brandy-faced beadle to drive Lazarus from the door, and waddle before Dives to the chief seats. A continental church is no white-washed pantile shop for paroquet costume, where a picture or statue could not be tolerated for fear of worldly pomp! But a temple enriched by the noblest talents of man for the honour of God, and opening its gates for him who has no other friend. I expected to find one great altar, gorgeously decorated, and no more; but found an altar enriched with carved wood, statuary, pictures, and precious marbles in every side recess, and between the pilasters all along the side aisles; so that service may proceed, without much interruption, in several places at once: and there are groups of poor market-people, who have laid down their baskets for a few moments (some still poorer), praying in oratories and dim recesses; and others prostrate at the door.

Thus far all is right, tho' the Romanists have not been wanting in other means of money-getting; but there are things more questionable. In the churches of Naples you see life-size figures of the Virgin, dressed out in the height of the fashion of the time when they were made; with stay-tight waists, and Bond Street hips, and rings on their fingers. When an image of the Madonna makes a procession through the streets it is preceded by soldiers with fixed bayonets, and a military band playing merry tunes. An image which I saw carried in Rome, with seven daggers in her breast, was, I think, borne by butchers — at least it was the butchers' costume, which is said to be that of the sacrificing priests of Jupiter. Like the Pagan house-hold gods, little ugly dolls of the Virgin and Saints under glass cases are kept in many of the houses; and votive offerings are hung in profusion in some of the churches, before the shrine of the delivering saint: horribly-painted little pictures too of remarkable deliverances from fire, drowning, or spirited horses, are sus-pended about them: and at a favourite shrine of Our Lady I saw innumerable knives stuck into leather thongs up the wall, which were the weapons of converted

[1] The Linnells lived at Bayswater.

assassins. You see parents lifting up their children to kiss the foot of a Saint. That of St. Peter in the Vatican, though of brass, is much worn.

No one was ever more cruelly or unexpectedly disappointed than myself with almost all the church music I have heard in France and Italy. During the con-secration of the Host, they play operatic music; and an organist once, who could not please the congregation by other melodies, played the air of 'Go to the Devil and shake yourself,' very much to their satisfaction. An eminent artist at Rome, who is also an organist, told me that after wearying a convent with fine music, he quite delighted them with 'Bumper Squire Jones.' At high mass I have heard the chant of the priest accompanied in the most frivolous taste; and when after loud music there comes an unaccompanied chant, the organ keeps the priest in tune with a loud shrieking note now and then, all the stops having been left open. The vocal choir of St. Peter's and the Sistine Chapel is very fine, but in the gallery of the former the leader stands in front beating time very energetically, and the cries of 'Piano! Piano!' are rather forte, and much too distinctly audible.

We saw the grand Easter ceremonies, and were several times within a yard of the Pope. We saw him wash the feet of the thirteen priests (whom he afterwards waits on at dinner, girding himself with a napkin), and after singing mass, bless the immense assembled multitudes from the façade of St. Peter's. This is a sublime spectacle – thousands of country people in their picturesque costumes, beating their breasts, holding out strings of beads, and awaiting, in breathless silence, the great benediction. When the Pope appears, all is hushed. He spreads out his arms over the people and blesses them; and then, all in a moment, the great guns of St. Angelo fire, the martial bands distributed over the piazza, strike up, and the bells of the city, which are silenced through Passion Week, ring out a peal. Before this, at the grand mass at St. Peter's, at the moment when the elements are con-secrated and all are prostrate, a slow, sublime harmony of wind instruments peals along from over the great western door, softened in this immense vault as in the open air. The dome, though much higher and vaster than St. Paul's, is not, in my judgment, nearly so sublime; and in sublimity and musical effect I think the grandest ceremonials of the Vatican are far short of our cathedral worship.

We found the scenery from Calais to Paris pretty tolerable in places, but the few villages on the high road looking very desolate and deserted. Indeed, through-out our French journey, excepting one single village in the south, all the little country places appeared dismantled and wretched, with not a gleam of cottage comfort. No rustic chimney 'between two aged oaks' (for forest timber we saw none till we came to Switzerland), no 'neat handed Phillis'; but houses in the taste of Walworth Common and Rotherhithe, only without, or with broken, glass, and tumbling to decay; and instead of ruddy ploughmen, ragged, sallow, blue-coated monsieurs; the whole looking as if it had been purged, not purified, through twenty, instead of three or four revolutions. This is not caricature, or an exaggeration of the *general* impression made on my senses. Our modern philosophers say, I believe, that our ideas come only through the medium of the senses, and really the sense of smelling is by no means an inactive agent in forming one's idea of France and Italy; nor the sense of feeling in the flea season, though happily for us, in Rome (to parody the kitten pie-man), *when frosts was in, fleas was out.* In Rome, where the bed-linen is shaken into the streets, we are told that in summer the fleas swarm you so as you walk that people are obliged to change their clothes when they come in; and at Naples, those little creatures which in the language of Dante are called 'pedoccii' so abound that they are sent home in the clean linen. However, a comb and soapsuds would sooner clean one of these, than the most stoic philosophy of the blue devils in lurid London. These vermin, though they certainly do not contribute to ease, are light and limber enough to grace the modern style of epistolary correspondence, which is said to derive most of its grace from facility of movement.

The fury and vociferation, and brutal, butt-end horsewhipping of French *diligence* drivers are a strange contrast to the quiet mastery of the 'Mr. Wellers' of old England. But the movement-note of one of our charioteers was very curious: while he was beating away with all his might, he was exciting his cattle with a tone exactly like the cooing of a dove!

We arrived at midnight in Paris, and put up with a most dismal-looking room in a great hotel whose gates were guarded by sentries. Nothing in travelling is so wretched as a night arrival in a strange city. We were surprised to find no soap on our wash-stands, but soon found it was an unheard-of luxury which we must buy and carry about with us through the whole journey. We found here several pretty nauseous examples of French filthiness.

At the risk of being every moment pushed down or run over, we began to explore Paris – were delighted with the Louvre, tho' the pictures are hung in the dark, but had not time for the Luxembourg. We were detained day after day by the shameful delays of the passport system, [and] our consolation was to creep now and then into the Louvre. We did not then know that by giving a few francs to the commissionaire of the inn, all would have been done for us. O! the physiognomies that I saw in the public offices! We were told that, some time since, the present *liberal* government took away from travellers on the frontiers the pistols which they carried for their private safety. The new king's soldiers form a guard of honour with a standard, over the graves of the so-called patriots who were killed in the act of dethroning the last monarch!

I shall not easily forget some grand old fortified and cathedral towns near the Swiss frontiers of France. We had just a glimpse of their grey fanes and mouldering battlements before we entered for the night, and left them before daylight in

[41]

the morning; which, when we looked back, we saw glimmering upon them in the valleys beneath. Sometimes the morning mist filled up the vales and plains like an ocean with its friths and bays; while the rising sun, striking upon the island-like summits and mountains, fired with living gold here and there an ancient village or city on their glowing ridges. Sometimes what seemed to be sky opened and disclosed a patriarchal village nestled among the pastoral downs, and glistening like silver or pearl through the rarer vapour; or the cloud would partially vanish or rise like a curtain, and disclose a champaign country at our feet; while, on either side of the road, the village people were brushing away the dew from the ripe vineyards, and piling up the purple treasure in baskets, or loading them upon teams of cream-coloured oxen.

Then came the wonders of Switzerland; while, winding up and down among vast green or furrowed slopes, or shaded by luxuriant forest timber, we saw the hoary Alps at sixty miles' distance glimmering like sunny clouds across the horizon – above them, greyer or more vaporous colour, and the Alps again! Lausanne sweeps down with its terraces and gardens to the margin of the great lake as it seems, though a mile intervenes, which is lost in the stupendous scale by which the eye measures everything: being filled with the giant forms on the other side.

On the hilly environs of the Lago Maggiore stands the statue of St. Charles Borromeo as large as a tower, with his hand stretched out over the country, as if blessing all beneath him. There is a staircase inside the statue, and several people can dine in his head. Mr. and Mrs. Richmond and Mrs. Palmer saw it, and a room where this blessed saint and servant of God was born, with a cast of his face, some of his hair &c. I did not, being plagued with heavy boots, and unable to ascend to these precious relics, which I reckon a great loss. I however saw the statue at a distance.

Our first sight of the lake was from a flower-trellised balcony at the inn, with the first crimson flush of dawn glowing behind its mountains.

Milan cathedral is a wonder of holy, Gothic, inspired art, and its dim religious light gilds the very recesses of the soul. It is the antithesis of the new Post-Office, and not very similar to the National Gallery.

But Florence is the 'city of my soul' – quaint, antique, stately, and gorgeous, and full of the gems of those divine and divinely inspired arts which, three centuries ago, lived there in wedded love with the old Platonic philosophy. Not the pot and kettle philosophy of The Useful Knowledge Society, beginning in steam-engines and ending in money and smoke, but visionary and ideal – the solid food of the soul. For money and beef are not, as people imagine, the solid things of the *mind*; but as unreal and unsatisfying to the immortal part, as a lecture on metaphysics would be to a hungry belly.

[42]

But what shall I say of Rome, of whose wonders a tenth part I have not seen, yet have seen what would fill a volume? Its churches are cathedrals and its Vatican larger than the city of Turin within the walls. Rome is a thing by itself which, once seen, leaves the memory no more – a city of Art which one had dreamed of before, and can scarce believe that one has really seen with these ocular jellies – to which London seems a warehouse, and Paris a trinket-shop. What must it have been in its antique glory? You can only look at its dazzling palaces, blazing in Italian sunshine, with your eyes half shut. Indeed, Italian air and Italian light, and the azure of an Italian sky, can scarcely be imagined in England. It spreads its magic over streets and houses, and invests the commonest objects with a peculiar beauty : but the people do not, I fear, plunge into the Tiber after athletic games as heretofore, or wash their carcases as we do every morning in cold water ; for they leave a wake of unsavoury odour behind them as they walk the streets, which are strewed with filth.

We have lately been exploring the wonderful environs of Naples, are now at Pozzuoli (Puteoli, where St. Paul landed), and hope soon to be in Rome for the winter.

I grieve to pass another Christmas without our family meeting. It made me sad last year to think of it, and I do earnestly hope, my dear John,[1] that we shall spend next Christmas but one together, and in company with our feathered friend, whom I have not forgotten, though my last sight of him was in your company. Green tea too, and the bookish evening have charms to draw me to England, where I hope we shall often enjoy them together. Pray write me a *long* letter . . . and tell me what delightful books you may have lighted on since my departure, and how little Willy and Samuel get on with their studies, which I long to know. Give my best love to them, and tell them they are not forgotten. Pray begin to write as soon as you get this, and write five minutes a day in a very small hand till the letter is full.

I saw Dr. Wiseman at the Easter ceremonies, with a purple gown and fur tippet, looking as sleek and fat as ever, and heard him preach once or twice. He has been getting up performances of Shakespeare's plays by his pupils of the English Academy. He sings, and is, I believe, fond of the arts.

I have been received with great respect by the first English artists in Rome, who were much pleased with a drawing I exhibited there. Mr. Richmond kindly introduced me to Mr. Baring, who gave me forty guineas for a view of the city, for his father's, Sir Thomas Baring's, collection. We met with a very pleasant and intellectual friend in a son of Sir Thomas Acland, who passed a good deal of time with us at Naples. I have said nothing about Mr. Richmond as I know he has been

---

[1] In addition to being addressed to Samuel Giles, the letter is inscribed 'To my dear Mrs. Giles, and to the rest of my dear cousins . . .'

in correspondence with you : indeed, I am very anxious to know where he is, as I do not much think he remained at Florence. Pray let me know, if you have heard. Do not forget between you to get me up a long letter. Give my love to all relations and friends, and believe me, my dear cousin, Ever yours affectionately,

SAMUEL PALMER.

When we were leaving Pozzuoli this morning, I saw a monk getting the materials for a dinner in a very cheap and ingenious way. He was presenting to all the old men and women in the little fish-market a glazed, coloured print of the Virgin to kiss, and was in turn presented by each with a small fish, which he carefully deposited in his handkerchief. I think in Billingsgate he would find himself as much out of his element as the fish themselves.

We have just heard from Mrs. Tatham (their aunt, at Naples), that the Richmonds are at Rome ; that Mr. R. is now quite well ; that Mrs. R. has continued all along in perfect health ; and that the Roman baby has cut six teeth and is a giant. Our children also are, I trust, pretty well. They are twins ; viz. Mrs. Palmer's drawings and my own. Dear little creatures ! They will I hope, support *us* instead of our having to keep *them*, which I hope will not be long ; for I desire speedily to launch them on the tide with a favourable gale. If they sail into the port of prosperity, people will begin to say, 'What a nice young man Mr. Palmer is. Ah ! I always said *he* would get on.' Perhaps now they say, 'Do you know that old fellow Palmer, with grey bristles on his head — he's an odd fish, isn't he ?' If I get on, I mean to live most temperately, but to establish a monthly Goose Club, with a few select friends who appreciate that noble bird. The morning to be spent in reading our old poets, the bird to be discussed about two o'clock, and vivid green tea to be brought in at four, and kept on the hob all the evening ; during which, over a blazing fire, we can talk over our old times at Greenwich and Shoreham, and have a little bit of Fletcher's *Faithful Shepherdess* now and then, or some of your old sophisticated Catholic books, dear John, which you must bring in your pocket. Tell me where you spent last Christmas Day, and whether you mourned, as I did, that the old family compact was broken up.

My dear Albert,[1] if you go on drawing, continue to study from the divine, eternal, naked form of man, even if you are driven out from the society of men, and obliged to pursue your studies in a hay-loft. Take the greatest pains to secure a beautiful outline, and study from the works of the finest masters. Every inch you gain in this way is a mile. The devout and holy study of the naked form purifies the imagination and affections, and makes us less pervious to evil temptation. Here, beauty is often the whited sepulchre of vice ; but in eternity that human form is, as it were, the body and symbol of goodness and truth. Seas may forsake their

---

[1] Here Palmer is apparently addressing another member of the Giles household.

channels, mountains be shaken to their base, but the eternal form of man will survive the wreck, and, as it existed from eternity in the Divine Idea, will flourish in immortal youth amid the 'clash of worlds.' I again subscribe myself, my dear cousin, Yours most affectionately.   S.P.

Now! Do you think I'm mad, all of you? If I am, come and be bitten, for the vaccination of artistic madness is a good specific against the small-pox of worldly vanities.

Excuse bad composition, for I write in great haste.[1]

Among the tasks which Samuel and Hannah had agreed to undertake in Italy was a series of copies of old masters for Linnell. At this drudgery, for it was nothing else, the young girl – she was, let us remember, only nineteen – spent an inordinate number of hours, days, weeks and months. Nevertheless misunderstandings arose between Palmer and Linnell concerning their progress and completion. Linnell wrote several times to Palmer, scolding him for what appeared to be his lack of interest in the copies. Palmer replied, pointing out that it was none of his fault that they were not being made as quickly as Linnell would have liked; that, indeed, Hannah had been working as hard as she could on the project. Later Linnell said that if Palmer had '*wished* them done they *would* be done'; to this Palmer was able to reply that he '*wished* them done and they *are* done'.[2] Later still, in reply to further accusations by Linnell, Palmer wrote of Linnell's 'fabric of suspicion' and suggested that when he returned to England they had better make it a rule not to talk on subjects about which they disagreed.[3]

Palmer was harassed, too, by money worries, despite the fact that he and his wife boarded and lodged in Italy for the equivalent of two shillings and sixpence a day. He tried to economise, some of his measures seeming pathetically irrelevant, as when he gave up snuff.[4] But such sacrifices were real enough to Palmer himself, and it did not help him when Linnell wrote messages to Hannah saying that she had been working too hard, that she should take things easier for a time 'and let Palmer pay, it does him good'.[5] It was with a *cri de coeur* that Palmer in another letter likened himself to a walnut tree which yields its full sweetness by bruising.

Palmer wrote to Linnell to ask his advice whether, in order to raise some funds, he should produce some 'little oil pictures and drawings painted in a day'. Linnell sensibly advised against this, saying it savoured 'too much of the practice of some who have stocked the market with cheap pennyworths of Art, to their own

---

[1] *Life and Letters*, pp. 201–8.   [2] Letter to Linnell, 30 June 1839. Ivimy MSS.

[3] Letters to Linnell, 16 August and 15 September 1839. In a very human letter to Palmer, written on 16 February 1839, Linnell wrote of 'the sweet temper' in which Palmer 'received . . . the asperities of my irritable fibre . . . I therefore calculate out of the abundance of your meekness . . . that you will make all possible allowances for me as you know how many things I have to attend to which distracts the mind & tries the temper.'

[4] Letter to Linnell, 30 June 1839. Ivimy MSS.   [5] Letter to Hannah Palmer, 26 April 1839. Ivimy MSS.

pecuniary disadvantage and degradation as Artists. . . . Better to teach for money, and take pains with some finished works for reputation.'[1]

Linnell's anxieties for the young couple are to some extent understandable. He must have seen Palmer as an ineffectual character, dissipating his time in elaborating theories and writing long letters and memoranda – on one of Palmer's letters to George Richmond the recipient wrote '5460 words'.[2] The Linnells must have felt some trepidation that their young daughter had married such a man and begun her married life with him in a strange foreign land. The fact that Linnell wrote to them once a fortnight is as much a sign of his restraint as of his anxiety. He could have written more often. And for a time the Palmers' letters did not get through to him regularly, which increased his own anxiety and that of his wife. But it must have seemed cruel to Palmer when Linnell suggested that on the couple's return Hannah should live with them for a time while Palmer occupied his own house, separated from her, to get it ready for their joint occupation. This would, wrote Palmer to Linnell, prevent him from painting some pictures he was planning. 'Now whatever others can do – *I* cannot attempt this in a desolate, dirty house, such as mine was during Mrs. Hurst's[3] administration – with clothes hanging to dry in the passage &c &c. Therefore I think – and indeed feel sure that the only way will be (the house having been made ready *before* our arrival) to go into it at once with Anny. . . .'[4]

Samuel and Hannah returned to England at the end of 1839, having been abroad for just over two years. They had, said their son, 'returned from a sunny and beautiful land to the dreary darkness of a London winter. Often and often my father spoke of the contrast between the brilliant skies and the marble buildings they had left behind, and the filthy Thames warehouses, looming through the fog in which they landed.'[5]

The artistic legacy of the Italian visit was strong in Palmer's subsequent work; it may be discerned in many passages in his etchings. We have remarked his predilection for horse-chestnuts. Now another kind of tree, the cypress, was to play a dominating role in his work. The beauties of the cypress were made abundantly clear to him by the magnificent specimens he saw at the Villa d'Este at Tivoli which, wrote Hannah in a letter to her parents on 16 December 1838, had with the pines, afforded Palmer a very rich drawing.[6] In a later letter (9 June 1839) Palmer writes that these cypresses are thought to be the finest extant.[7] The drawing mentioned by Hannah is probably one now in the Paul Mellon collection (Plate 21). It is a powerful work, related both in execution and style to certain

---

[1] *Life and Letters*, p. 68.   [2] Stirling, A. M. W., *The Richmond Papers* (London, 1926) p. 13.
[3] Palmer's housekeeper after the death of Mary Ward.
[4] *Life and Letters*, p. 72. The original letter is now in the Ivimy MSS.   [5] *ibid*. p. 72.
[6] Ivimy MSS.   [7] *ibid*.

works of the Shoreham period, such as a fine pencil study of ancient trees in Lullingstone Park (1828). The cypress drawing was to provide Palmer with inspiration for many details in his later work, as for example in a magnificent view of the Villa d'Este, now in the Ashmolean Museum, in the wood engraving of the Villa from the Cypress Avenue designed by Palmer for Dickens's *Pictures from Italy* (1846 – Plate 22) and, as we shall see, in several of his etchings.

The Palmers did not return to England like conquering heroes, and indeed found their money difficulties at home as bad as or worse than those they had experienced in Italy. To add to his income Palmer gave lessons, and apropos of this he wrote, in 1840, this entry in his memorandum book : 'Supposing lessons stop, and nothing more is earned – avoid snuff, two candles, sugar in tea, waste of butter and soap. . . . But it is more difficult at present to get than to save. Query. Go into the country for one month to make little drawings for sale?' So despite Linnell's previous advice, Palmer was still toying with the idea of making potboilers.[1]

On the back of some rough drafts of letters in the collection of Miss Joan Linnell Ivimy are various calculations concerning Palmer's income and expenditure, which give a vivid idea of his straitened finances. They are given in full in Appendix A.

Palmer referred again to his income in a memorandum book entry made during 1842

Income, God willing, of 1842✝. He giveth food to all flesh, for His mercy endureth for ever . . . Our professional experience, 1842. February 3, I went to the British Gallery, and found both my pictures and one of Anny's rejected. March. Mr. Ruskin and others were shown our drawings. Mr. Nasmyth was to name me as a teacher to Admiral Otway. I offered Miss B—, Addison Road, to teach one pupil for 10s. per annum. [This was a school.] Went to British Artists, and found one picture hung near the ceiling, another rejected, and Anny's *Job* rejected. Mine were the same pictures I sent to the B: Gallery, for the new frames for which I had paid £5 8s.[2]

Palmer was also dissatisfied with his medium. He wanted to paint in oils, but was forced by circumstances to concentrate on water-colours. For one thing he could not spare time to practise the less familiar medium, and at least the time spent on water-colours produced some income. For another thing he found the oil medium difficult to handle. As his son wrote, his 'oil pictures of this time . . . were weak and timid to a degree surprising to those who are familiar with the crisp touch, glowing colour, and bold impasto of the best Shoreham panels'.[3] Palmer later lamented the discouragement he had met, presumably from Linnell and

---

[1] *Life and Letters*, p. 73. [2] *ibid*. [3] *ibid*.

Hannah, 'and the golden dreams he had dreamed under the bright Italian noon faded away into the cold realities of a disappointed life.'[1]

But Palmer's failure to overcome all these difficulties was probably as much the fault of his own personality as of extraneous influences. It is possible that he was wrong in any case to want to use oil colours. Water-colour, and later etching, were well suited to his muse and it would be difficult to imagine his subjects expressed even half as well in another medium. In any case, whether he liked it or not, he was confirmed in the water-colour medium when he was elected in 1843 to an Associate-ship in the Old Water-Colour Society.

The artist Robert Hills (1769–1844) was secretary of the Water-Colour Society when Palmer was elected. It is of interest that Hills sometimes signed his work 'Extollager',[2] and may have been a member of Palmer's circle. If so, his letter of 14 February 1843 informing Palmer of his election[3] was extremely formal and so was Palmer's reply to it, a draft of which exists :[4]

Sir/ I beg leave gratefully to acknowledge your letter of the 14th & to express my deep sense of the honor which the Members of the Society of Painters in Water-color have been pleased to confer upon me.

I have ever felt that an artist can receive no encouragement so unequivocal as the favorable judgment of those who stand at the head of his profession & I trust that the privelege of being allowed to exhibit my works in your gallery on the same walls with those of the most eminent painters while it animates every hope I may entertain of future excellence will confirm those habits of incessant and devoted study which lead to its attainment.

I shall be much obliged Sir if you will express to your Society my warmest acknowledgements of their kindness & my solicitude to deserve it –

I have the honor to be Sir

Your most obedient

Samuel Palmer

Robert Hills Esqre

Palmer made several sketching expeditions into different parts of the country, and also made extended visits from time to time – Thatcham in Berkshire, Princes Risborough in Buckinghamshire, Margate, Guildford, Cornwall and North Wales. During these expeditions and also during the time he spent at home, he wrote pages of memoranda about his theories on art. This must have taken up hours of his time,

---

[1] *Life and Letters*, p. 74.

[2] Cf. page 26. And see Hardie, Martin, *Water-colour Painting in Britain. II The Romantic Period* (London, 1967) p. 160.

[3] Ivimy MSS.   [4] *ibid.*

10. The Morning of Life
Etching. $5\frac{3}{8} \times 8\frac{1}{4}$ inches. State III
Ashmolean Museum

11. The Bellman

Etching. $6\frac{9}{16} \times 9\frac{3}{16}$ inches. State IV

Mrs. Raymond Lister

12. The Lonely Tower

Etching. $6\frac{1}{2}$ to $6\frac{9}{16} \times 9\frac{3}{16}$ inches. State IV

Mrs. Raymond Lister

13. Opening the Fold *or* Early Morning
Etching. $4\frac{5}{8} \times 6\frac{15}{16}$ inches. State VIII

Mrs. Raymond Lister

14. The Homeward Star
Etching. $3\frac{15}{16} \times 5\frac{15}{16}$ inches. State II
Ashmolean Museum

15. The Cypress Grove

Etching. $3\frac{15}{16} \times 5\frac{15}{16}$ inches. State II

Ashmolean Museum

16. The Sepulchre

Etching. $3\frac{15}{16} \times 5\frac{15}{16}$ inches. State II

Mrs. Raymond Lister

17. Moeris and Galatea
Etching. $3\frac{15}{16} \times 5\frac{15}{16}$ inches
Mrs. Raymond Lister

time that would have been better spent in drawing and painting. There ran through his notes an account of dissatisfaction, as here :

Monday, April 17, 1843. — Taking-in day at the Water Colour. Thoughts as to my next year's painting if my unworthy life be spared. Try to make my things first Poetic ; second Effective.

POETIC	EFFECTIVE
By doing subjects I love and greatly desire to do. BRITISH ; ROMANTIC ; CLASSIC ; IDEAL.	By studying phenomena in the country, laying the great stress upon small — very small sketches of effects ; always making, at the same time, at least a small pencil outline of the matter ; and that I may not be solicitous to produce showable pictures in the country, let me now, at home, do all I can for the next Water-colour exhibition.[1]

Here and there when the grumbling and dissatisfaction had for a moment been laid aside are notes that throw a vivid light on Palmer's artistic aims and endeavours : 'To get vast space, what a world of power does aerial perspective open ! From the dock-leaf at our feet, far, far away to the isles of the ocean. And thence — far thence, into the abyss of boundless light. O ! what heavenly grays does this suggest !'[2] Sometimes a short sentence or comment comes like an illumination. What a wealth of associations arise for instance in the brief phrase, 'The tender moonlight seen at Mr. Calvert's.'[3]

Samuel and Hannah Palmer's first child, named Thomas More after the sixteenth-century lawyer, statesman and martyr, was born on 27 January 1842. Palmer had for long admired Sir Thomas More and that other Catholic martyr of Tudor times, John Fisher, Bishop of Rochester. Palmer had hung their portraits in his room at Shoreham to 'frown away vice and levity and infidelity'. Their second child, a daughter, Mary Elizabeth, was born in 1844, and their third child, Alfred Herbert, later to be Palmer's biographer, was born in 1853.

After 1845, Palmer's income improved somewhat, though it came chiefly from teaching. But he did sell a few pictures and drawings for an average of £16 apiece. He also received fees from other sources, such as twenty guineas from Messrs. Bradbury and Evans for illustrations for Dickens's *Pictures from Italy*. But teaching was a chore, as may be seen in this extract from a letter written to

[1] *Life and Letters*, p. 77. [2] *ibid.* p. 79. [3] *ibid.* p. 82.

D [49] S.P.E.

Hannah on 14 June 1847: 'What use I could have made in the country of these three weeks of fine weather! If I could but stand the loss of the first disentanglement from teaching I think it would be a hundred times overpaid; but it is full of difficulties.'[1] Yet he could not afford to throw his teaching aside; in the following year, 1848, two-thirds of his income was derived from it.[2]

On 15 December 1847, six months after the foregoing memorandum was made, tragedy struck at Palmer. His three-year-old daughter died that day at twenty-five minutes to six in the afternoon. This event brought upon him 'an intense, ceaseless, and insufferable torture. . . . His grief was also the harder to bear by means of his almost childish inability to restrain it. He had to go about his work and to keep his teaching engagements with eyes bleared and a voice often choked by sorrow.'[3] Edward Calvert tried to comfort Hannah and Samuel in their distress, and for a period spent every evening with them.

The Palmers' Marylebone house had become associated in their minds with the tragedy and they determined to move out of it. The following March they therefore moved into a cottage, 1A, Victoria Road, Kensington. In December of the same year, 1848, Palmer's father died, aged seventy-three.

In the period following this there was a further deterioration in the relationship between Palmer and Linnell, mainly because of religious differences. Unfortunately Hannah's sympathies for her husband seem for a time, under her father's influence, to have diminished also.[4] In one of his letters to her, Palmer sends her a lengthy statement of his religious views, 'That we may never have in future to misspend time in the deplorable mischief of religious controversy.'[5] Of this, A. H. Palmer wrote, 'The circumstances which led to the writing of the foregoing words were not without their influence on his subsequent history, and led to others which served to embitter the more effectually, much of his future life.'[6]

It was in the midst of such unfortunate relationships that Palmer turned to etching. The 'Old' Etching Club had been founded in 1838 by a group of artists which included Thomas Oldham Barlow and C. W. Cope, who were always considered by Palmer to be important mentors in his early etching days. It was a serious professional club, the members of which were expected to produce a given number of plates periodically; failure to do this led to expulsion. Royal Academicians were proud to belong to it. Palmer was received as a member in 1850, his probationary plate being 'The Willow' (Plate 1). The minute book belonging to that period records that 'the minutes of the preceding meeting having been read and confirmed as correct, the club proceeded to ballot for Palmer, who was unanimously elected and introduced to the club'.

'The Willow' was not an unqualified success, as Palmer was admonished by

[1] *Life and Letters*, p. 85. [2] *ibid.* p. 88. [3] *ibid.* p. 86.
[4] Grigson, *op. cit.* p. 136. [5] *Life and Letters*, p. 90. [6] *ibid.*

Thomas Creswick for ruling some of the lines in the sky instead of making them freehand.[1] Nevertheless the members must have realised the potential power of Palmer's work from this small plate. His subsequent plates more than confirmed their confidence in him.

In part it must have been Palmer's dissatisfaction with painting that helped to turn him to etching. We have it on his son's authority that he would have gladly abandoned painting altogether in favour of etching if it had been practicable to do so.[2] Palmer himself wrote, in a letter to P. G. Hamerton :

'The Little Corporal' would have upset two or three dynasties while I have been debating with myself whether or not it is possible for me to find time for the etching. Inclination says, 'If you can't find the time, *make* it ;' and a subject has occurred to me which would be the very thing for the purpose.

If this kind of needlework could be made fairly remunerative, I should be content to do nothing else, so curiously attractive is the teazing, temper-trying, yet fascinating copper. But my etchings consume much time, and I am not alone in discovering that, like the cash absorbed by bricks and mortar, the final amount often doubles the estimate : and this time has to be withdrawn from commissions which are really lucrative. I can get 100 guineas for quite a small drawing which does not occupy nearly the time of some of my etchings ; but I am purchasable, perhaps, not only for one, but for a small series of larger etchings, which are in contemplation, on terms which would be just to my family . . .[3]

Palmer in fact was able to spend comparatively little time on etchings. He completed four small plates in 1850, published one more in 1852, two in 1857 and one in 1858. Two others he had begun by 1860–1, but he completed no more until 1879. Between that year and 1881, the year of his death, he worked on seven more plates, four of which were completed by his son and published posthumously. We shall deal with all of these in greater detail in the next chapter.

For the moment let us return to our account of Palmer's life. After living for three years in Victoria Road he moved into a house in a nearby cul-de-sac, 6, Douro Place, 'about the most complete antithesis to his ideal of a residence that could have been devised. It was a hideous little semi-detached house, with a prim little garden at the back and front, and an ample opportunity of profiting by the next door neighbour's musical proclivities.'[4] There was no proper studio and Palmer had to be content to work in a drawing room which for its outlook had a row of houses on the opposite side of the street. Sometimes he strained his neck out of an attic window to see the effect of a fine sunset. The room in which he

---

[1] Hardie, Martin, *Samuel Palmer* (London, 1928) p. 19.   [2] *Samuel Palmer A Memoir*, p. 30.
[3] *Life and Letters*, pp. 314–15.   [4] *Life and Letters*, p. 101.

worked was simply, even poorly furnished. He 'foreswore nice furniture and other fittings for his study, in favour of rough, clumsy shelves, primitive palette racks, mended chairs, and decrepit tables . . . everything was a protest against what he was pleased to call "Cursed Gentility" '.[1] None of this was lost on dealers who came to buy his work, for they noticed his apparent near-poverty and paid him accordingly. He was no business man, and did not bother to haggle with them. 'He still not only put a very low price upon his very best work, but often failed to get even that; and he was indifferent to the time he bestowed in ripening a drawing, even after it had been exhibited, bought and paid for.'[2] Painstaking though he was in this respect, his etchings claimed his first interest. In a book of designs he wrote the following sentence, which followed a number of resolutions concerning his drawings and paintings: 'Have an eye to the above this year, D.V., but let the ETCHING be the point of most painstaking.'[3]

During the period of Palmer's life from 1848 to 1858 he made four visits to Devon and Cornwall. He wrote enthusiastically about the time he spent there. As will be seen in the following extract, his etchings were much in his mind at this time. 'This would be a thing to do very leisurely; no luggage, but one spare shirt. Sketching portfolio with *thin* plate-paper, and Richard and Wilson's thin brown paper, which would weigh lightly. In pocket, case of pencils and black and white chalk, and light little box for reserve black and white chalk, and the three chromes, and blue and browns for slight indications of local colour on the brown paper. This, on the whole, I find the most rapid method of sketching . . . I ought to watch the operations of husbandry. The MONTHS would make a good book of etchings.'[4]

Sometimes, in letters and notes written by Palmer on these expeditions, there is an echo of the Shoreham spirit, as when he wrote this during a visit to Wales: 'In exploring wild country I have been for a fortnight together uncertain each day whether I shall get a bed under cover at night; and about midsummer I have repeatedly been walking all night to watch the mystic phenomena of the silent hours.'[5]

Palmer was near-sighted and because of this he always carried with him a pair of large, round neutral-tint spectacles. He is shown wearing them in a portrait by Henry Walter (Plate 24). Another visual aid he sometimes used was his 'Claude glass', which he mentions in his 1824–5 Sketchbook. It was a coloured or dark spyglass, providing a diminished and subdued reflection.[6] The device was named after Claude, because of the similarity between his pictures and the effect it produced.

[1] *Life and Letters*, pp. 130–1.   [2] *ibid*. p. 102.   [3] *ibid*. p. 103.
[4] *Life and Letters*, p. 106.   [5] *Life and Letters*, pp. 75–6.
[6] A Claude glass is illustrated on page 397, Vol. CXLIII, No. 3703 of *Country Life*.

We have already noticed an instance of the eccentricity of Palmer's appearance. This became accentuated as he grew older. He wrote that it seemed to him 'that while nothing is more silly than eccentricity for its own sake, few things are more pernicious than the dread of being peculiar'.[1] He certainly observed this precept himself. Like his contemporary, Philip Henry Gosse the naturalist, he endeavoured to make himself look like a parson (Plate 25). He generally wore, 'on state occasions, a loose and lengthy broadcloth coat of a rather peculiar cut, and full of pockets so ample that, at a pinch, they easily engulfed a sketching outfit. A double-breasted waistcoat, buttoned high and close over the formal folds of an old-fashioned white cravat, added to a clerical appearance which was sufficiently great to cause a country clergyman, on one occasion, to request, through the clerk, his assistance in the service.'[2] He wore the biggest hat he could buy and the hatter addressed the parcel in which it was sent to the 'Rev. S. Palmer'.[3] He patched his own shoes and garments when they became worn. Later in life he was never seen outside his studio without being wrapped in his shawl, and he admitted that when travelling on railways he appeared 'swathed like a mummy'.[4] If the weather was cold he wore two sets of underclothing, and if it was particularly severe he wore in addition two pairs of trousers.[5]

Some of his eccentricities brought reminders of Shoreham. The 'Ancients' had sat up late drinking green tea, watching natural phenomena and reading poetry. Later in life Palmer still kept late hours and wrote 'blessed Green-tea-time winds us up for *Macbeth* or *Hamlet* and ecstasy'.[6] He began habitually to talk to himself and to address imaginary people – 'Mr Jackson', 'Mr. Jinks', and 'Mr. Jick'. He gave names to the things he used – his paraffin lamp was 'Nancy'.[7] He grew weeds in his garden and tended them as lovingly as if they had been the rarest flowers.[8] Yet his attitude to some things was sensible enough. He tried continually to debunk pomposity and gentility, as when with mincing gestures he wore what appeared to be a gold ring, only to be disclosed to some bourgeois visitor as a curtain ring.[9] And he soundly and contemptuously condemned what he called the tight lacing curse, by means of which the ladies of his time distorted their figures into the shape of hour glasses. 'Yes, I say *CURSE*, and I mean it, and wonder how Kingsley[10] could have done his duty so thoroughly and at the same time have kept his temper so well. . . . He is amused at the peals of laughter with which a tight-waisted female would have been greeted by the ladies of Attica. I have the honour to have long shared this ludicrous vision with Mr. Kingsley, and to have imagined the very fish-women of the Piraeus pelting her with sea-weed.'[11]

[1] *Life and Letters*, p. 131.   [2] *ibid.* p. 131.   [3] *ibid.* p. 136.   [4] *ibid.* p. 146.   [5] *ibid.* p. 136.
[6] *Life and Letters*, p. 209.   [7] *ibid.*, pp. 145–6.   [8] *ibid.* p. 134.   [9] *ibid.* p. 146.
[10] Charles Kingsley, author of *The Water Babies* etc. He had published in *Good Words* an article in which he castigated tight lacing.
[11] *Life and Letters*, p. 306.

Certain odd psychological manifestations in Palmer's character were apparent also. He was for instance preoccupied with flagellation, as is illustrated in many of his letters. 'I believe if an angel were to come down and whip us every Monday morning, it would give us a fillip, and do us all much good.'[1] 'O! for the leisure to contemplate it an hour daily with knotted scourge in hand to lash myself into some semblance of . . . efficiency.'[2] 'I think that he should have been moderately whipped who said that orthodoxy was . . . the sin against the Holy Ghost.'[3] 'I have yet to learn that, unless after flagellation, the human skin is much granulated.'[4] 'The pernicious folly of those whom the Devil has persuaded to banish the rod from the nursery.'[5]

Many more examples could be quoted. The foregoing date from 1838 to 1881 and therefore cover a large portion of his life, showing that flagellation was in his mind for many years. With it went a strong streak of puritanism, as when he wrote of 'pure' music — music, that is, without words — as playing 'the wanton in a luxurious effeminancy which a wise commonweal would forbid'.[6]

In June 1854 Palmer was elected to full membership of the Society of Painters in Water Colours. He continued to subject his work to elaborate theorising and criticism, and in 1859 he made another of his tabulated summaries:

1859. What must I do to attain excellence?
Increase what I love.
What do I heartily love? Much! Figures of antique grace and sentiment, and rich picturesqueness.

———

Intense depth of shadow and colour. Mystery, and infinite going-in-i-tiveness.

———

The focus, a well-head of dazzling light.
The utmost deep and heaped up Devonshire richness.
EFFECTS. Midsummer glowing Twilight, and rising moon, with trees of intensest depth . . .

———

Moonlight with firelight.

———

Supply Deficiencies. Where am I weak? (or rather alas! where am I *not* weak?) Design figures vigorously. Consult model *early*. Paint them neatly.

Conduct picture, so that from the first it may be sightly for its state. At the moment when I would shudder to show it let me pause and ask, 'why?' I ought to keep the shadows and half-tints flatter. Let me try to make the getting in exactly resemble OIL painting, with that broad suggestive smear in the half tints and in the landscape part of the lights. *Painted*, not glazed; as *e.g.* yellow ochre and emerald green for smooth grass — laid smooth, so as just to cover the paper. Even in skies — still more

[1] *Life and Letters*, p. 201.   [2] *ibid.* p. 277.   [3] *ibid.* p. 299.   [4] *ibid.* p. 333.   [5] *ibid.* p. 402.   [6] *ibid.* p. 318.

Sunsets. Dawn. Silver Sunrise.
Sunset through trees.
Cloudy, fresh, dropping, spring morning. One focus of cream white cloud.

in landscape, lay the TINTS as nearly as I can of the relative intended depth, like a woodcutter – leaving the gradations for the finishing.[1]

Again his notes sound echoes of the Shoreham years, and again his etchings seem to satisfy him more than his paintings: 'Try a silver morning, perhaps sun-rise. Rich twilight. . . . By models or otherwise, avoid looseness in the focuses. Think of subjects which have for some time been discontinued, as sheep under trees, or in fold; descending stubble-fields with village in deep distance, but always with figure story. . . . Why did the moonlight etching[2] please everybody? Partly by structure and effect; partly because the matter was not above compre-hension, whilst it was a kind of matter which I most strongly feel. N.B. It grew out of a most simple thing – houses at Margate with bars of moonlight. Could I find among my *effects* things as simple which would develop?'[3] On the outside of a paper portfolio in 1860 he wrote, 'Thoughts on RISING MOON, with raving-mad splendour of orange twilight-glow on landscape. I saw that at Shoreham. Above all this, one pinnacle might catch the fire of the last sunlight.'[4]

He could achieve such effects in his etchings. 'The Rising Moon' (Plate 7) 'The Weary Ploughman' (Plate 8), 'The Herdsman's Cottage' (Plate 3), all completed before 1860, show them, and they become even more apparent in the great etchings of his later years, such as 'The Bellman' (Plate 11) and 'The Lonely Tower' (Plate 12). Here there is a confident expression, often missing from water-colours painted at about the same time. 'A Harvest Field' for instance (Plate 26) is competent work, but it is far removed from the visionary fervour of the Shoreham studies, and falls, too, far behind the magnificent studies of the Villa d'Este cypresses. The etchings seem, while he worked on them, to have claimed most of his truly creative powers. One reason for this is, as we have already remarked, that Palmer was happy in the technique of etching, whereas he was unhappy working in water-colours, continually lamenting his inability to find time to express himself in oils. Indeed his water-colour technique was in many ways conditioned by the technique of oil painting, such as where he laid on his colours with a palette knife in a thick impasto mixed with gum. This was apparent even in the Shoreham drawings – in such a work for instance as 'In a Shoreham Garden'.[5] These bastard techniques are now proving their shortcomings, for many of the pictures on which they were used are cracking and flaking away and

[1] *Life and Letters*, p. 113. [2] 'The Rising Moon' (Plate 7). [3] *Life and Letters*, p. 112.
[4] *ibid.* p. 113. [5] *circa* 1826; Victoria and Albert Museum.

it is doubtful if they can be saved. Though his etching technique was also in some ways unconventional it was never stretched to such limits as these.

Another technique used by Palmer was 'drawing upon wood'. Most book illustrations in those days were wood-engravings. In preparing for these, the surface of the plain boxwood block was made ready by a craftsman, and on this the illustrator made his drawing either in pencil, pen-and-ink, water-colour, or, more rarely, chalk. A journeyman engraver then worked on it, reproducing the artist's drawing in terms of engraving. The original drawing was thus destroyed in the process. Later it was possible to sensitise the surface of the block and to reproduce the artist's drawing on it by photography. Until this time, however, the artist, as in the case of Palmer, drew on the wood. It was for Palmer a stage in an engraving technique, and one would have thought that with his love for etching, it would have appealed to him. Perhaps it did. But the results disappointed him and he seems to have demanded from the engravers more than they were able to give.

Some books containing illustrations of this kind by Palmer are *A Poetry Book for Children*,[1] *Sacred Allegories* by William Adams (1856),[2] *A Book of Favourite Modern Ballads* (1859), *Household Song* (1861) and *Legends and Lyrics* by A. A. Proctor (1865).

Notwithstanding Palmer's disappointment these illustrations have a certain charm. That for 'The Hermit' from *A Book of Favourite Modern Ballads* shows a figure looking across a lake towards a church tower, with a sickle moon above the horizon. Its sentiment is not unlike that in 'The Lonely Tower' etching (Plates 27 and 12). Palmer's two illustrations for this book are printed in colour. This was made possible by the superimposition of several different blocks, which were engraved by Edmund Evans.[3] Palmer's nine illustrations for *Sacred Allegories* contain many of the Shoreham elements – sheep, crescent moons, sunrays – and a memory of the Villa d'Este cypresses. One of them seems to look forward to the etching 'The Sepulchre' (Plates 28 and 16). These illustrations, which were engraved by W. T. Green, W. Measom, and H. Harral, were praised by Gleeson White who wrote : 'The amazing quality of the landscapes by Samuel Palmer stood even the test of enormous enlargement in lantern slides, when Mr. Pennell showed them at his lectures on the men of the sixties ; had W. T. Green engraved no other blocks, he might be ranked as a great craftsman on the evidence of these alone.'[4]

During these years one of Palmer's dearest ambitions was to provide his son Thomas More with the best preparations for life that were within his power. This led him to try all kinds of compromises in his work in attempts to increase his

---

[1] I have never seen a copy of this book, nor do I know its date.

[2] There was a second edition of this in 1859.

[3] For an account of this great engraver see *The Reminiscences of Edmund Evans wood-engraver and colour printer 1826–1905* (Oxford, 1967).

[4] *English Illustration 'The Sixties' 1855–70* (London, 1897) p. 103. See also Appendix C.

income so that he could pay for the best possible education for him. That he was over anxious to achieve this is apparent from the fact that he gave the child his first drawing lesson when he was two years old.[1] Palmer's earnest attitude towards his son may be seen in the following letter, written to the boy in 1859 when he was seventeen. It is full of laudable and good advice, but one feels that no sense of fun or high spirits could penetrate such a relationship.

Hastings, *June*, 1859

My Dear More. A man with no *aliud agere* is, as you say, likely to be a mere animal; but so far as his worldly interests are concerned, he is often a very efficient animal. I allude to what are called 'the plodders who get on'.

A first-rate man is one who has taken quite as much pains as the plodder to attain excellence in some one thing, and has done *that* all the better for his general curiosity and varied information. The danger with young men is this, that general knowledge – a superficial smattering of many things is a much easier affair than first-rate excellence in any one thing; it does not call out those peculiar energies and that discriminating refinement of judgment which can alone arise from a grapple with some one worthy subject.

As to a *livelihood*, concentration is all important. Where there are so many competitors there must be genuine excellence to ensure (D.V.) a slice of the bread and cheese which society deals round to the *workers*. We can work only according to our strength, but so far as that reaches, the great thing is to do our *very best*.

Emerson says, 'Genius is patience.'[2] Patience and painstaking are indispensable to *high* excellence. When you have the happiness to know any one who is first-rate in his way, you will find him, like Mr. Brown [head master of Charterhouse] harping upon 'accuracy and elements' 'elements and accuracy.' This is what gives position in life. More or less of this defines the income and prospects of the scholar – makes the difference between the head master and the usher. There are much higher views of the subject, but I will now close my sermon.

. . . I am glad to hear you have the Beethoven, and the more so, as it is a work complete in itself. I did not think the microscope scheme bad. I doubt whether even upon the back of 'a flea as big as a mastiff,' you could hop quite so far as into the invisible world. You will best do that, by watching your heart morally as well as physically. 'Keep thy *heart* with all diligence; for out of it are the issues of life'; and alas, alas, of *death* also, the physical again, being a true type of the moral.

But to return. The microscope would have been used comparatively seldom; the music will (D.V.) very often amuse you. But *do* mind to secure your present great opportunity of being a good classic. It is far too great a thing to be done by

[1] *Life and Letters*, p. 119.
[2] According to Lord Beaconsfield the saying is Buffon's. See Tancred. – Note by A. H. Palmer.

[57]

halves ; and unfortunately, if we become but half-people, the halves will not become wholes, like those of the polypus.

How grand must be the Gregorian music at All Saints', with such an organ ! Were I young again, I should like to sing in that choir. How happy must Sir Thomas More have felt (laying aside the Chancellor's gown on Saturday) to don the chorister's surplice next day in old Chelsea Church, where, if you remember, we have before now worshipped together. 'Blessed are they that dwell in thy house : they will be still praising thee.'

In architecture, in music and the other arts, in society, in the different intellectual orders of men, you are now seeing a great variety. When we rise in thought by steps and stages from the trifling to the sublime, we scarcely perceive how far they are asunder ; but put them side by side, and they are like 'Pop goes the weasel' on a cracked fiddle compared with the Gregorian choir at All Saints'.

If you come across any one who talks very freely about other people and laughs at them, *do* remember, if only from prudential motives, that to one who has his way to hew through the world such a habit is absolute *suicide*. Such a habit is both hateful and treacherous ; treacherous because the material of ridicule and scandal is often filched from its very victims in the confidence of social intercourse — perhaps under their very roof ! While we listen to such tattle we are ourselves, perhaps, furnishing material for amusement at our expense. Nasty things are sometimes done by otherwise very nice people. Hence the danger. We should try to embody in ourselves a portion of each *good* thing we see among our friends, and so, as we roam, collect honey everywhere. The fly, unlike the bee, settles with satisfaction on every little heap of filth and refuse. Sometimes there is a good deal of drollery and even wit mixed up with what is wrong, and that makes it the more dangerous.

. . . It seems to me, that all the eminent and considerable men have laid up *while young* a large stock of solid knowledge, which they have afterwards embellished by eloquence and fancy. But they had to make their ginger-bread before they could gild it. In light literature, think how much must go to make a book like *The Caxtons*. I do not allude to quotations, but to the texture of the general fabric. You may get your 'trimming' from books of reference, but the wool or the silk must be homespun.

If you have time to write a letter of decent length, like the last, I should be glad of it. Incidents and adventures are pleasant. When you have something to tell, and feel that you should like to tell it, here I am.

Let me advise you amidst all you meet with, gay or grave, pleasant or irksome, to remember that there is also RIGHT and WRONG — *never to forget that*; and that whatever present satisfaction many of the blessings of Providence throw in our way *gratis*, yet, as Mr. Brown quotes to you, 'Nil sine *magno* vita labor ededit mortalibus.' I remain, dear More, Your affectionate father, S. Palmer.[1]

As time passed Thomas More showed some promise as a scholar; in consequence Palmer hoped to send him to a university with a view to his later entering the church. However, by the time he was nineteen and had become head boy at his school, he had begun to show signs of great physical weakness and Palmer determined to take him into the country for a period to recuperate. With this in view he hired, early in 1861, a farmhouse 'High Ashes' at Abinger, lying on the slope of a valley between Holmbury Hill and Leith Hill in Surrey. He settled his family here before returning to London himself.

Hopes rose and fell as Thomas More showed signs of recovery, only to be followed by relapses. Finally his weak frame could fight his illness no longer and he died on 11 July 1861. Palmer was stricken down with grief and 'rushed from the house in bewildered agony and never re-entered it. One of the doctors, seeing his critical condition, drove him in his carriage to the house of his brother-in-law, Mr. James Linnell, at Red Hill, and he saw Abinger no more from that day'.[2] The same evening he wrote to Calvert:

My dear Calvert, As you are the *first* of my friends whom I sit down to make partaker of my sorrow, I will not wait for black-edged paper, which is sent for.

You I take first, for you were first in kindness when dear little Mary was called away, and your *kind, kind* heart will be wrung to hear that at our lodging at High Ashes, near Dorking, on Leith Hill, my darling Thomas More left us at a quarter to six. It was effusion of blood on the brain.

I can write no more, dear Mr. and Mrs. Calvert, and do not know where I shall be for the next few days. Broken-hearted, I remain Your old, old friend, S. Palmer.

My poor wife is at High Ashes, where the dear fellow died.[3]

Linnell was present when Thomas More died and when Palmer was taken away by the doctor. He tried to persuade Hannah to leave the undertaker to bury her son. It was in some ways sensible advice, but it did not show much understanding of her feelings. 'Let the dead bury their dead,' he said.[4] It did not prevent Hannah from attending her son's burial beneath a yew tree in Abinger churchyard, though her husband was so broken by grief that he could not accompany her. During the following November he wrote to a friend that the first snow had fallen on Thomas More's grave, and adds, 'Is it not a comfort to find that his numerous manuscripts, and the contents of his private desk meant for no eye to see, are as unsullied as that driven snow? Yes! he will lie to-night under his new winter

[1] *Life and Letters*, pp. 223–5.   [2] *ibid.* p. 123.   [3] *ibid.* p. 230.   [4] Grigson, *op. cit.* p. 136.

shroud. . . . There is no sensation in the grave, so it is a foolish fancy; but I have always felt it so very sad that, while *we* are warm by our winter fire-side, those precious limbs, mouldering though they be, of our lost dear ones should be far away from us, unhoused and in the damp, cold earth, under the wind, and rain, and frost. Thrice happy those to whom the grave is a golden gate, and who *know* that "though worms destroy this body", yet in their flesh they shall see God. . . . But what am I writing? the snow has set me off, for "I cannot choose but weep, to think they should lay him i' the cold ground".'[1]

Palmer's grief was so overwhelming that even his art seemed to have died within him. 'My loss,' he wrote, 'has made me so incapable of *personal gratification* from external objects, that what is called a beautiful view gives me no more real pleasure than the contemplation of a kitchen sink.'[2] But he had to make a living to support himself, his wife and remaining son, and he felt it an additional duty to use his talents. But, he wrote, 'How can I make works which will cheer others when quite cheerless myself? Perhaps thus. 1st, choosing themes I *loved*, for I love no art themes now; 2nd, very simple and massive in effect; 3rd, getting in whole effect (after the figures are well designed) at a heat; 4th, sufficient model realization; 5th, delicate pencilling. Can etching be made productive? Vanity of vanities.'[3]

Thus in his extremity of grief he saw his beloved etching as the one possible technique through which he might still express something worthwhile. But it was mere vanity to think it could make him an adequate income. Years later, writing to Hamerton, he gives a reason for this. 'It is *my* misfortune to work slowly, not from any wish to niggle, but because I cannot otherwise get certain shimmerings of light, and mysteries of shadow; so that only a pretty good price would yield journeyman's wages.'[4] Indeed Palmer was forced for a time to abandon etching altogether because of the demands of his water-colour compositions. It must have been a hard decision.[5]

The Palmers decided to move from Kensington as soon as possible after their son's death. They moved first to a small lodging on Redhill Common, which they used as a centre from which to search for something more permanent. In September 1861 they found a small cottage in Reigate, near to Linnell's house. The choice was made mainly to meet Hannah's wish to live near her parents. 'But my father,' wrote A. H. Palmer, 'would certainly have preferred almost any other.'[6] The cottage was damp and Hannah was soon in the grip of rheumatism. This forced her to go to live for some months with her parents at their house, Redstone Wood, while Samuel was left 'to a nearly solitary and inconceivably miserable sojourn'.[7]

There seems to have been some family bitterness. This was hinted at by Palmer's son when, having written of his parents' religious controversies, he added: 'Per-

---

[1] *Life and Letters*, pp. 230-1.   [2] *ibid.* p. 125.   [3] *ibid.* p. 125.   [4] *Life and Letters*, p. 377.
[5] *Palmer Memoir*, p. 30.   [6] *Life and Letters*, p. 125.   [7] *Life and Letters*, p. 125.

sonally, he had little inducement to linger at Red Hill, and he did no more than pay intermittent visits from London to his family.'[1] Probably, for the time being, he kept the Kensington house and spent most of his time there, hoping that by his close proximity to the centre of the art world in the capital, he would have better opportunities to maintain and improve his income. The reference is, however, somewhat cryptic. No further allusion to it appears in any of A. H. Palmer's writings, nor, so far as I have been able to ascertain, in Samuel Palmer's letters, none of which appears to have been written from London during the Redhill period.

In May 1862, the Palmers moved again, this time to Furze Hill House, Mead Vale, Redhill. It was a genteel 'Gothic villa', and Palmer, some of his old sense of humour returning, suitably nicknamed the rooms. The drawing room became 'The Saloon'; one bedroom, 'The Boudoir'; another, damp, bedroom, 'Bronchitis Bower'; a little cupboard on the ground floor, 'The Butler's Pantry'. But it was a considerable improvement on the damp cottage they had recently occupied, and stood in a pleasantly wooded garden in which whitethroats and nightingales sang.

Here, in time, Palmer overcame much of his sorrow. He was able, too, to give thought and time to the education and career of his surviving son:

As early as I can remember I had been promoted (sitting in my baby chair) to help him to fasten in his drawings with paste and paper, for the exhibition, an opportunity for mischief and mess which he turned into an elementary lesson in painstaking. Toys were very rare, but I scarcely missed them, for there were a hundred little things to do, connected with art, which he managed to make amusing. Few would have patiently borne with the bungling of childhood in like matters, but it was an important point in my father's method of teaching to set me things to do that really wanted doing, and to point out that disastrous consequences would follow failure. By this teaching, and by his own example, he gradually fixed in my mind a conviction that whatever is worth doing at all is worth doing well, and that few things can be done in a worthy manner without patience. Elements, Accuracy, Method, Patience, Humility — these were the cardinal points in my father's teaching.

He attached great importance to the regular lessons, which included Latin, arithmetic, drawing, and English; but these were administered in doses which, nowadays, would be considered infinitesimal.[2]

Palmer continued to read widely, especially Shakespeare, Chaucer, Scott and

---

[1] *Life and Letters*, p. 90.

[2] *ibid.* p. 129. A. H. Palmer was, as a child, made to carry a parasol as a guard against sunstroke. (*Victoria and Albert Museum Catalogue*, p. 15.)

Dickens. He disliked most games, considering them an interference with conversation, but he made an exception of backgammon, which he often played during winter evenings. Like a good Victorian he observed Sunday strictly, attending morning service when his health allowed him to. He dreaded things that interrupted his daily routine, and of such things spring-cleaning was what he dreaded most. He actually left home while it was in progress, either visiting London or his friend J. C. Hook R.A. at Churt, near Farnham in Surrey. Apart from this he visited Hook annually, either at Churt or at Witley, his other residence.

Palmer was not untouched by the religious upheavals occasioned by the scientific discoveries and thought of the nineteenth century. For instance he reacted violently to Darwinism. 'He who gainsays or slights the miracles of holy Scripture,' he wrote to his friend Bryan Hook, 'is a fogy; he is a stickler for ancient Pharaoh whose heart was hardened, even after the seven plagues. He who says there is no Devil is a fogy – a stickler for the old Sadducees who said there was "neither angel, nor spirit".

'There is nothing new in infidelity; suppose that I read in some new book that men were once baboons; it is merely a slight improvement on Lord Monboddo who, more than a century ago, fancied that men once had tails.[1]

'The vamped up arguments against miracles were familiar to me when I was fourteen, and perhaps I thought it manly to be a bit of a free-thinker! But at that time, unbelievers were honest enough to avow their unbelief: some of them now profess to be advanced Christians! What is Rationalism but infidelity with a fraudulent label? . . .

'This is no laughing matter to *us*, but will not He that dwelleth in Heaven laugh them to scorn who fancy that they have given the go-by to a faith which commanded the supreme reverence of such intellects as those of Augustine, Anselm, Bacon, Milton, Dante, Barrow, Pascal, Newton? Would these men have thrown away their Bibles because coral-reefs took a long time in forming, or somebody fancied himself the grandson of an ape?'[2]

Palmer was not a great disputant. So far as was consistent with his self-respect he would agree rather than argue with an adversary. But when he did choose to take up an argument he could be tenacious and like Blake he would not hesitate to use paradox to extricate himself from a difficult argument.

In 1863 sprang up a fruitful friendship between Palmer and Leonard R. Valpy, a London solicitor who had bought Palmer's small drawing 'Twilight: The Chapel by The Bridge' at the Old Water-Colour Society's winter exhibition. Valpy suggested that a small improvement could be made to the drawing by

[1] Lord Monboddo's study *Of The Origin and Progress of Language* (1774) placed apes on a footing almost equal to humans.

[2] *Life and Letters*, pp. 312–14.

toning down the light in the chapel windows and Palmer readily agreed to make the adjustment. In Valpy's words, their 'sympathy expanded and acquaintance ripened into friendship'.[1]

Valpy asked Palmer if he might see anything on which the artist was then working and that was particularly expressive of what he called his 'inner sympathies'. Palmer answered that he may, writing :

Now only three days have passed since I did begin the meditation of a subject which, for twenty years, has affected my sympathies with sevenfold inwardness ; though now, for the first time, I seem to feel in some sort the power of realizing it.

It is from one of the finest passages in what Edmund Burke thought the finest poem in the English language :

> 'Or, if the air will not permit,
> Some still removèd place will fit,
> Where dying embers[2] through the room
> Teach light to counterfeit a gloom,
> Far from all resort of mirth,
> Save the cricket on the hearth.'

The lower lines a companion subject out of doors.

> 'Or the bellman's drousy charm
> To bless the doors from nightly harm.'

I am trying the former small — the size of your *Chapel*. The student, in his country, old-fashioned room, meditating between the lights : the room dimly bronzed by the dying embers (*warranted without 'RAYS' !*) and a very cool, deep glimpse of landscape, and fragment of clouded moon seen through the lattice, just silvering the head and shoulders : the young wife in shade, spinning perhaps, on one side of the fireplace. Should I displease myself with it, the 'dying embers' may revive within my own fire-grate ; if the contrary, it will give me much pleasure to show it you *by and bye*.

I carried the Minor Poems in my pocket for twenty years, and once went into the country expressly for retirement, while attempting a set of designs for *L'Allegro* and *Il Penseroso*, not one of which I have painted (! ! !), though I have often made and sold other subjects from Milton. But I have often dreamed the day-dream of a small-sized set of subjects (not however monotonous in their shape yet still a

---

[1] *Life and Letters*, p. 149. Valpy was solicitor to John Ruskin and Lady Palmerston.

[2] A. H. Palmer added this footnote to MSS.: 'My father quotes from memory, and although he knew *Il Penseroso* by heart, not only writes "dying" for "glowing", but (as the context shows) evidently thinks the word enhances the poetic sentiment.'

set ; perhaps a dozen or so), half from the one and half from the other poem. For I never artistically know 'such a sacred and homefelt delight' as when endeavouring in all humility, to realize after a sort the imagery of Milton.[1]

Valpy asked Palmer if he would produce a set of drawings such as he mentions in the foregoing letter, illustrating Milton's minor poems. About April 1865, after some discussion, it was agreed that Palmer should make eight such drawings, each measuring 28 by 20 inches, on themes from *L'Allegro* and *Il Penseroso*. It was to prove to be a pleasant commission for Palmer, and out of the drawings stemmed some of his noblest etchings – 'The Bellman' (Plate 11), 'The Lonely Tower' (Plate 12), and elements of 'The Early Ploughman' (Plate 9). The drawings were published posthumously in 1889, with some others for *Comus*[2] and *Lycidas* in *The Minor Poems of John Milton*.

Of the etchings that stemmed from this work, Palmer wrote : 'The etching dream came over me in this way : I am making my working sketches a quarter of the size of the drawings, and was surprised and not displeased to notice the variety, the difference of each from all the rest. I saw within, a set of highly-finished etchings, the size of Turner's *Liber Studiorum*, and as finished as my moonlight with the cypresses ['The Rising Moon'], a set making a book, a compact block of work, which I would fain hope might live when I am with the fallen leaves.'[3]

At about this time Palmer installed his own printing press and had his son taught the technique of printing from copper plates. His teacher was Frederick Goulding, one of the greatest of all copper-plate printers ; the technique of taking impressions from etched plates is a craft as skilled as that of actually etching them. Goulding enjoyed the respect of the foremost etchers of his day.[4]

But let us return to the Milton drawings. The work on them proceeded slowly with appreciation and criticism from Valpy, some of the latter leading to 'a few decided collisions of opinion. . . . Although Mr. Valpy had definite notions of his own as to the rendering of Milton's imagery, they were somewhat realistic ; and where they differed from his friend's, he was compelled to throw the reins upon the neck of an imagination which he found so unusually strong. Both men were in earnest, neither disdained to learn from the other. . . .'[5]

Palmer had only just finished work on the Milton drawings when he died in

---

[1] *Life and Letters*, pp. 254–5.

[2] These had been exhibited in 1855 at the gallery of the Old Water-Colour Society. *The Minor Poems of John Milton with twelve illustrations by Samuel Palmer Painter and Etcher* (London, 1889) p. xi.

[3] *Minor Poems of Milton*, p. xvi.

[4] Goulding was born in 1842 and died in 1909. He served an apprenticeship as a printer and was at one time an assistant to James McNeill Whistler. He set up his own press in 1877. In 1890 he was elected by the Royal Society of Painter-Etchers as their first master printer. See Appendix B.

[5] *Life and Letters*, p. 151.

18. Late Twilight
Pen and brush in sepia, mixed with gum and varnished. $7\frac{1}{16} \times 9\frac{3}{16}$ inches
Ashmolean Museum

19. Harvest under a Waning Moon
Wood engraving. $1\frac{1}{16}$ to $1\frac{1}{32} \times 3\frac{1}{32}$ inches
Ashmolean Museum

20. Pastoral with Horse-chestnut
Water-colour and body-colour. $13 \times 10\frac{5}{16}$ inches
Ashmolean Museum

21. The Cypresses at the Villa d'Este, Tivoli
Black chalk, water-colour and gouache. $12\frac{1}{2} \times 9$ inches
From the collection of Mr. and Mrs. Paul Mellon

22. Wood engraving after Palmer from
the opening page of *Pictures from Italy*
by Charles Dickens. The Villa d'Este
from the Cypress Avenue
$5\frac{1}{8} \times 2\frac{7}{8}$ inches

23. Antique gem. From *Handbook of
Engraved Gems* by C. W. King

24. Portrait of Samuel Palmer by Henry Walter
Water-colour and pen. 21 × 14 inches
Trustees of the British Museum

25. Photograph of Samuel Palmer in old age
From *Samuel Palmer a Memoir* by A. H. Palmer

26. A Harvest Field

Water-colour. $12\frac{1}{16} \times 21$ inches

27. Wood engraving in colour after Palmer for 'The Hermit' by Beattie from *A Book of Favourite Modern Ballads*
$2\frac{3}{4} \times 3\frac{3}{4}$ inches

28. Wood engraving by W. T. Green after Palmer. 'They could only look up to the stranger with tearful eyes.' From *Sacred Allegories* by Rev. William Adams
$4\frac{1}{2} \times 3\frac{3}{4}$ inches

1881. The slowness of his progress may be accounted for partly by his painstaking methods – unusual even for a Victorian artist. On 21 November 1867 he wrote, 'While I was touching on the sheep in *The Lonely Tower*, all of a sudden, I don't know why, the whole seemed to come as I intended, so I packed it up in a paper and string to make it difficult to get at, lest I should spoil it. In this state, a few breathings, after we have had a final look at it, will be precious.'[1] Twelve years later, in 1879, he wrote to Valpy, '. . . I loved the subjects, and was willing to be a loser in all but the higher matters of Art and Friendship. I do not in the least complain that I have lost a thousand pounds by them. It was my own act and deed. In the same time, I could have made thrice the number of telling and effective drawings of the same size, but I considered your taste and feeling so much above the ordinary standard that, in order fully to satisfy them, I have *lavished time without limit or measure*, even after I myself considered the works complete.'[2] Four months before he died Palmer was still writing of these drawings and working on two of them – 'The Eastern Gate' and 'The Prospect' from *L'Allegro*. Of the former he wrote, 'I am anxious to do my all for it, whatever that may be, as it seems to have impressed several persons more than anything I have done . . . but I wish to bring all to a close.'[3]

The Milton series contains some of the finest of Palmer's later water-colours. His skies, his magnificent sunrises, crescent moons, and clouds – some of them the alto-cumulus which he had loved to paint in his Shoreham drawings – are truly poetic visions. At last Palmer seemed to be sloughing off the non-visionary skin that enveloped his post-Shoreham paintings. He was returning to the poetry of the earth, to the true beauties of its natural phenomena – the poetry of moonlight and starlight, the darkness of dew and the pregnancy of the soil. These works do not have the immediacy of the youthful works painted at Shoreham, but they are different, the work of what Rupert Brooke would have seen as 'that unhoped serene, that men call age'.[4]

Another undertaking that occupied Palmer during roughly the same period as his Milton drawings was his translation and illustrations of Virgil's Eclogues – what his son described as 'an ill-fated project'.[5] Palmer had loved the poems of Virgil for many years and had for long wanted to translate them into English verse. He had worked on translations from time to time, and had been assisted in this by Calvert, who was an enthusiastic classicist. He was as painstaking in this work as in his painting and etching. His manuscript became in time 'so interlined, erased, and cut about for the insertion of slips of new matter, that but little of the original remained'.[6] The translation was almost complete by May 1872, by which time he

---

[1] *Life and Letters*, p. 151 [2] *Life and Letters*, p. 152.
[3] *Minor Poems of Milton*, p. xviii. [4] 'The Dead'.
[5] *Life and Letters*, p. 155. [6] *Life and Letters*, p. 155.

had sought the advice of Hamerton, who suggested that the verse was more likely to succeed if some illustrations were added.

Although Palmer had hoped that his translation would stand on its own merits, he accepted this advice. He therefore drew ten subjects which he hoped would be reproduced, without loss of detail and freshness, by some photo-mechanical process. But in this he was to be disappointed, and finally Hamerton suggested that the only satisfactory procedure would be for Palmer to make original etchings. Palmer again accepted Hamerton's advice, but in the event he completed only one etching, that known as 'Opening the Fold' (Plate 13), for he commenced work on them only in 1880, a few months before he died. Four others were left partly completed and were finished by his son (Plates 14 to 17). 'Opening the Fold', the four other etchings and ten drawings were all reproduced in *An English Version of the Eclogues of Virgil*, posthumously published in 1883. 'Opening the Fold' was also separately published by the Fine Art Society just before Palmer's death.

Many of the Virgil illustrations fall short, artistically, of the Milton series, though 'Opening the Fold' and 'The Cypress Grove' are exceptions to this. The etching for the First Eclogue (Plate 14) shows, as much as any other work of his later life, a return to the Shoreham vision. He had those times in mind in connexion with the Virgil illustrations, for in a letter to Hamerton, written on 26 January 1872, he wrote: 'If Blake were alive and I could afford it, I would ask him to make a head-piece to each bucolic. How exquisitely he would have done it we know, seeing that perhaps the most intense gems of bucolic sentiment in the whole range of art are his little wood-cut illustrations to Phillips' [*sic*] *Pastorals* in Dr. Thornton's book. They seem to me utterly unique.'[1]

In some of his correspondence with Hamerton concerning the Virgil illustrations, Palmer affords us an insight into the problems and techniques of his etching:

May, 1872: Knowing by old experience what time an etching insidiously consumes before I can make the effect ring, I doubt whether the etchings of such subjects could be managed under from twenty to thirty guineas each according to size...

January 13, 1879:... My etchings consume very much time, because, though I aim above all things at simple arrangements and fewness of masses, yet the progress is analytic, and matter aggregates within matter till the copper looks as large as a half-length canvas. An artist *dares* NOT flinch from his own conceptions, whether in the first impulse of invention, or its innumerable vibrations, widening like the circles when a stone is thrown into the water. Now all this is, I believe, the veriest castle-building, and doubtless I shall, if writ at all, be 'writ in water-

[1] *Life and Letters*, p. 323.

[66]

colours', instead of that delightful, durable, printer's ink, with a strong touch of brown in it ...

and in a notebook he wrote :

Process 1874 D.V., For etching get first the great, leading, *pathetic* lines, having first obtained the same in the figures. Work from the great leading lines and to them recur. Make friends of the white paper.[1]

Palmer wrote a long introduction to the Virgil, 'Some Observations on the Country and on Rural Poetry'. It is somewhat verbose, though full of lofty ideals. Yet the actual translation shows little awareness of the content of Virgil's original. The Second Eclogue, for example, a song of pederastic love, was transformed into a version in which 'Corydon, neglecting his affairs, laments the coldness of Galatea ; but coming to himself, rebukes his own folly in wasting time and substance upon an unrequited attachment'.[2] This is the Eclogue singled out by Byron in the couplet :

> But Virgil's songs are pure, except that horrid one
> Beginning with 'Formosum Pastor Corydon'.[3]

Palmer treated such matters euphemistically. He kept Calvert's delightful little wood engraving of a rustic wedding night, 'The Chamber Idyll', in an envelope.

Palmer's declining years brought an increase in bad health, especially of asthma which had always plagued him. But he was not senile. His sight and hearing remained unimpaired, and when he was confined to bed, as was often the case, he kept a table beside him on which he could work. When that was impossible he read. 'The true book-lover,' he wrote, 'is all tiger. He tears open his prey, and slakes his drought with huge draughts from the jugular.'[4] Sometimes he amused himself with problems in algebra and arithmetic. His income had improved and he was able to live more comfortably than before, but he made no attempt to put his work aside.

There came, too, a return to tenderness in his relations with Hannah, who was always with him, attending to his wants and guarding his health. Sometimes she read aloud to him, especially from Bunyan and from collections of sermons. Sometimes they drove together in a fly into the countryside, admiring its beauties, but lamenting the incursions of the railway. Palmer looked back sometimes to the days of his youth, and turned over relics of the Shoreham days. Sometimes he

---

[1] *Life and Letters*, p. 158. [2] *An English Version of the Eclogues of Virgil*, p. 25.
[3] *Don Juan*. Canto the First XLII. [4] *Life and Letters*, p. 163.

walked slowly into his garden, supported by his stick, to gaze on some of his beloved wild flowers. But however his increasing age affected him, his etching cupboard was always kept in order.

The last winter of his life was spent almost entirely in bed, where, in a heavy flannel overcoat, he continued to work on his Milton and Virgil illustrations. In May he was taken seriously ill, and died on the twenty-fourth of that month, with his old friend George Richmond reading prayers beside his bed.

Among those who were present at his funeral was Richard Redgrave. 'Sissy and I went down to our dear friend Samuel Palmer's funeral,' he wrote. 'It was a nice spring day. He is laid to rest in the pretty churchyard at Reigate. We met Richmond and his son at Charing Cross, and they travelled with us. Palmer was a great master of light and shade, as well as a fine colourist. We always keep his letters, they are so characteristic of the man, and so witty and delightful. He and his wife have been kind friends to my girls.'[1] To this we may add a sentence from his son's account of the event: 'Just above us a skylark joyously sang till, as the last words of the service died away, it dropped silently into the long grass.'[2]

[1] Redgrave, F. M., *Richard Redgrave*, p. 350.   [2] *Life and Letters*, p. 168.

III

The Vision Returned

Among the effects in Palmer's study was a cupboard in a corner set aside for etching. It was, according to his son, a holy of holies, and he described it as 'a rough, home-made cupboard, standing on a chest of drawers; containing, the one a veteran set of tools and a stock of copper plates, new or in progress; the other, a collection of early and touched proofs of former plates, some favourite etchings by other hands, and a few relics of the childhood of the son and daughter who were dead'.[1] Here Palmer spent some of the happier days of his middle and later life.

Before we consider the etchings, let us look briefly at the technique of the art as it was practised in Palmer's time. First a polished copper plate[2] was covered with acid-resisting wax ground, of which there are several kinds. With a steel needle the etcher scratched his design in reverse through this ground. The plate was then immersed in a bath of acid which bit the exposed face of the metal without affecting those portions still covered with wax. When the plate had been immersed for a period sufficient to bite the lines to the required depth, it was removed from the bath and some of the lines stopped out as necessary. That is to say, any lines which were considered to be bitten to a sufficient depth were at this stage painted over with wax. The plate was then replaced in the bath for a further period and after-wards removed for further stopping out. The process was repeated several times until sufficient variety of tones had been achieved. The wax was then removed and a proof taken. The etcher judged the progress of his work from this, and having ascertained which lines needed strengthening he laid a new ground, made further immersions and took further proofs until the desired result was achieved. Lines could be removed by burnishing the plate, or could be added or strengthened by an engraver's burin, especially during the final stages.

It was at the successive stages of immersion and proofing that the various 'states' of an etching arose. Thus lettering might be added at one stage, perhaps removed at another. Certain lines might also be added to some stages or removed at others. (Today the technique of etching has many refinements unknown to the old etchers.)

In printing, the technique of which is still much the same as it was in Palmer's time, the plate is heated and printing ink spread over it with an inking roller or

<hr>

[1] Palmer, *Memoir*, p. 28.   [2] Sometimes zinc or steel was used.

dabber. The ink is then wiped off the surface, first by a pad made of canvas, muslin or some other suitable material, and then by the palm of the hand, which has previously been rubbed on a block of whitening. The plate is again slightly warmed and a process known as retroussage follows. This consists of taking a piece of folded muslin and applying it under its own weight to the inked lines. This brings up the ink in them, increasing their strength where desired. In this way the quality of an etching may be greatly enhanced. A piece of dampened paper is then laid on the plate, which is passed with it through a press. The ink in the lines is thus transferred to the paper, giving the finished etching.

Palmer described his early exercises in etching as 'a scramble of uncertainties from beginning to end'.[1] Uncertainties there were, accidents happened, and bad luck sometimes dogged him. 'I spent,' he once wrote, 'several days working and proving in London in a ghastly frame of mind, owing, for once, not to my own clumsiness, but to the detestability, both as to thinness and quality, of the old, scraped, Club copper on which [my etching] was done. I gave myself up for lost on Saturday at 5.30, but, by a desperate perserverance, had singed the last neck of the hydra by 6.15, and hope to send you soon, one of the very best impressions. . . . My wretched plate bent up like an earwig disturbed in an egg-plum.'[2]

This was 'The Morning of Life' (Plate 10), which had been etched on a plate thinned down by removing a previous etching. It is not to be wondered at that the thin plate curled in the printing press.

Palmer could use even accidents to his advantage : 'I remember once spending a whole day in nearly burnishing out a sky that was overbitten. The perverse acid *would* bite skies and nothing else ; but being spared to attempt another, I humbly trust to go half through the copper.'[3] This was 'The Skylark' (Plate 2), and it gave what A. H. Palmer called 'the delicate upward flush of early dawn over thin vaporous cloud . . . the result of the day's elbow-grease directed, not by knowledge of any etching technicality, but by knowledge of one of the most beautiful effects in nature'.[4]

Stopping out Palmer used extensively. To Hamerton he gave his views on this as applied to the drawing of clouds : 'I am inclined to think that, in cloud-shadowing, long lines should be avoided, and that the short ones would naturally vary some-what in direction, and that cross hatching should be used very sparingly. In complicated skies, I doubt whether much can be done without frequent stoppings-out and rebitings. The most precious thing I was ever taught seems to be this ; "One day of stopping-out is worth five with the needle ;"[5] and this, quite irrespective of the style of work as to more or less pronunciation of line. Directly we

[1] *Life and Letters*, p. 99.   [2] *Life and Letters*, p. 99.   [3] *ibid.*
[4] *Life and Letters*, p. 99.   [5] The remark was repeated to Palmer by Barlow. See p. 83.

think of a real *organized* sky, the whole condition of work is changed, and quite a new scale of study and force elsewhere is demanded to support it.'[1]

He returns to the problems of stopping out and other aspects of technique in another letter to the same correspondent :

I can quite sympathize with you about etching uncertainties. My standing grief has been the unaccountable stopping of the biting, after two or three – sometimes after one stopping-out ; and it may be useful to know that you are subject to this with the Dutch mordant ; which, never having tried it, I hoped was reliable, till the other day I learned the reverse from one of our finest etchers.

Your thin ground difficulty obliges you to do what seems to me the best thing possible, viz. to remove the ground after completing the outlines and the organic markings. I should like an outline as deeply bitten as those in the *Liber Studiorum* ; and believe that if we were to make an etched copy of a bit of near landscape out of one of Albert Dürer's wood-cuts, of the same width of line, and then, on a new transparent ground, to add what we wished of shade, the lines would scarcely be too powerful to support them. And the purely liquid quality of all shadow, to which anything like richness of texture is destruction, coming over the textured richness of the lines would give that fulness of quality which in art, as in everything else, can result only from the union of opposites. He is great, says Pascal, who touches the poles with his grasp.

Let any one look at a fine impression of Albert Dürer's Holy Family going through the wood, with the palm-tree on the left, and think what a comfort it would be to have such a preparation ready bitten on the copper, the ground removed, and a transparent one laid on for beginning the shadows. But somehow or another, I fancy we have all of us more or less the notion that because an etching should be spirited it should be done in a hurry. I grant that there is a sort of vigour and a very agreeable texture got in this way, which delights the eye for a short time, but beyond which the work never grows upon us : but Rembrandt's, many of whose etchings are, in the leading points, very highly finished, which he was constantly revising, sometimes to the extent of organic changes, retain their hold long after the first ocular pleasure is over.

I am no great believer in etching direct from nature ; or in doing anything but through the medium of studies. Callcott[2] told me he thought that a picture done out of doors must needs be false, because nature is changing every minute. But if a pen and ink drawing is made out of doors, there is more left for selection, and all that is most attractive can be faithfully transferred to the copper ; very near objects [being] worked at the same hour of each day. Grand tree-trunks and the like seem

---

[1] *Life and Letters*, p. 315. [2] Sir Augustus Wall Callcott (1779–1844), landscape painter.

[71]

excellent subjects; but distances and mountains never know their own minds ten minutes together, so we are obliged to have two drawings, one of the parts – one of the chosen phenomenon seized at the moment.[1]

Palmer did not use retroussage extensively as he felt it destroyed the quality of his line. As his friend Hook remarked, 'Lose your line and you lose your light.'[2] To Barlow, Palmer wrote:

For myself I doubt whether etching in the old sense of the word is not almost superseded by the new art of *retroussage* added by the printer upon a comparatively slight fabric. Sometimes it has been very effective, but, in most instances, is so inferior to linear etching as to become quite another art: but then, as it produces an effect quite as satisfactory to the public eye in about one fifth of the time, it beats linear etching out of the market. It seems to me that the charm of etching is the glimmering through of the white paper even in the shadows; so that almost every-thing either sparkles, or suggests sparkle. Now this is somewhat like the effect of a purely white ground under an oil painting. The *demonstrable* difference may be small, but the real deterioration of a dark ground is universal; and, not to quote irreverently, is 'a darkness that may be felt' if it cannot be proved. Well, *retroussage*, if not kept within narrow bounds, extinguishes those thousand little luminous eyes which peer through a finished linear etching, and in those of Claude are moving sunshine upon dew, or dew upon violets in the shade.[3]

Above all, Palmer's etched work was achieved by great painstaking. 'Those who have seen him sitting, sable in hand, hour after hour behind the tissue paper, pencilling in varnish silver cloudlets round a moon; or have seen him revelling in the ferocity of the seething mordant with which he sometimes loved to excavate an emphatic passage will not wonder that he achieved only thirteen etchings; and they will think, perhaps, that the measure of his celebrity, in this his favourite branch of art, is well deserved.'[4]

Even framing and mounting received minute attention from Palmer. Of one of the Etching Club issues of his work, he wrote to Cope (15 March 1880): 'One subscriber sent his copy back & has had the sunk mounts enlarged so as to show a little of the plate paper around the etching. I heard that the mounts which came close up to the etching were thick and cast a shadow upon them. But again I hear that this is the FASHION, & that one of the crack etchers approves of it – *Still* I fear that such an anomaly must retard the sale of the work, if it is still proceeding. . . .'[5] In a letter to his son of 22 October 1880 he asks him to arrange

---

[1] *Life and Letters*, pp. 316–17.   [2] *ibid*. p. 100.   [3] *Life and Letters*, pp. 365–6.
[4] *ibid*. p. 100.   [5] Ivimy MSS.

for some framing to be done 'getting the allowance as I have to give them away', and complains of the difficulty in obtaining patterns : 'In all other trades there are little books of samples or diagrams, but here, one has to put one's head into one sack and one's hand into another & draw out what comes.'[1]

Palmer himself saw in his etching something that put it in a different category from the other visual arts, something that took it close to literature :

ETCHING seems to me to stand quite alone among the complete arts in its compatibility with authorship. You are spared the dreadful death-grapple with colour which makes every earnest artist's liver a pathological curiosity. Take, for instance, only a unit of the milliard — the painting of but one bit of human flesh under one given influence of light and atmosphere. Well I remember Mulready's saying to me, 'To get one quality of flesh is comparatively easy ; to get two is difficult ; to unite three is very difficult.'

Etching does not necessarily demand more than individual or local chiaroscuro, and the crayon will seize brilliant phenomena.

But the great peculiarity of etching seems to be that its difficulties are not such as excite the mind to 'restless ecstasy,' but are an elegant mixture of the manual, chemical and calculative, so that its very mishaps and blunders (usually remediable) are a constant amusement. The tickling sometimes amounts to torture, but, on the whole, it raises and keeps alive a speculative curiosity — it has something of the excitement of gambling, without its guilt and its ruin. For these and other reasons I am inclined to think it the best comptu exponent of the artist-author's thoughts.

(Quite abruptly, as it occurs to me, I would suggest that it is sometimes best, when you have much near matter, not to etch delicate sky or distance at first, but to put them in after two or three bitings : you then are in no terror, and can overbite and get a good rattling first proof. My best first proofs were those which quite frightened me ; and I foolishly began softening, instead of laying a ground for intense, dark lines like those in the Liber Studiorum, which would soon have brought the first biting to reason. If you work from an organized effect in your little sketch, you don't want so much to see your effect on the copper.)[2]

In another letter to Hamerton, Palmer contrasts mezzotint with etching to the former's detriment :

You mention mezzotint in connection with etching. It seems to me that, in some degree, the deep shades of mezzotint differ for the worse from those of etching, in much the same way as the shadows of an oil picture painted on a half-tint ground from the shadows of one on a white ground. I mean when a year or two has done its work with the former. The cases too are analagous as to time ; mezzotint, beautiful as it is, and low-toned grounds, bad as they are, being more rapid and cashy. One of the finest qualities of etching seems to me to be a certain luminousness even in its dark shades ; in all but the very darkest : and, if this be a 'bull,' it is the fault of the fact.

Etching, regarded from your point of view, does seem to be the finest of the metal methods ; and it can easily be shown to be better than wood-cutting, which lacks variety in its dark shadows, though the sparkle of its light is joyous. Then let its flashes illuminate etching ; let all be inclusive and cumulative. What is any art but that which genius has made it by extending its boundaries, while criticism demurred at every venture? Whence this strange gratification in scraping art with a potsherd, and paring the eye-lids of Regulus ?[1]

Yet Hamerton, who was an authority on the history and technique of etching, saw Palmer's work as a departure from true etching technique, though none the less because of that work of the highest quality. 'Samuel Palmer,' he wrote, 'is less a true etcher than a noble painter expressing himself with the etching-needle, and however marvellous is the work which he has done on copper, I am inclined to believe that the kind of engraving which would suit his genius best is not etching, but mezzo-tint.'[2] We may be thankful that Palmer did not heed this. As we have seen, etching was to him a sufficiently lengthy and painstaking operation. If he had indulged in the intricacies of mezzotint it is doubtful if he would have completed a single plate.[3] Nevertheless Hamerton was well aware of the power of Palmer's work. He said, 'There is more feeling and insight and knowledge in one twig drawn by his hand than in the life's production of many a well-known artist.'[4]

Later Palmer returns to the subject in another letter to Hamerton : 'The fact is that outline, with its *local* shadows, can be etched rapidly ; not so that mystic maze of enticement ideal *chiaroscuro*, of which I think you will agree with me that etching is the best exponent. Mezzotint is the more obvious ; but, however well done, it lies in some degree under the disadvantage so fatal to oil-paintings, of a dark ground, by which the pictures of a whole nation have been disfigured ere now. Like that cruel Othello, it puts out the light and then puts out the light ; eclipsing the sun before it closes the shutters. Though, with Ben Jonson's witches, etching says to a shadow, here and there, "Deep, O deep, we lay thee to sleep ;" yet, like those deepest of the deep yet clearest of the clear early Flemish pictures, there is the virgin white of the gesso ground behind.'[5]

---

[1] *Life and Letters*, pp. 344–5.   [2] *Etching and Etchers* (London, 1868) p. 144.

[3] In mezzotint a copper plate is uniformly roughened all over, and the lighter parts of the plate are obtained by scraping away the rough surface so as to give the right tones. The finished effect is rich, but the method is long and laborious.

[4] *Print Collector's Quarterly* (Boston, Mass., 1913) Vol. III, p. 207.   [5] *Life and Letters*, p. 376.

But it is time for us to examine in detail the individual etchings. We will first take the earliest and smallest of them, Palmer's probationary plate 'The Willow' (Plate 1). In this a large willow tree grows from a bank, first horizontally then vertically, over a river on which a swan swims. A little farther off two cows stand in the shallows. In the distance is a church tower. The sky is calm and little breeze seems to disturb the foliage of the tree, though at the top right-hand corner its leaves appear to be lightly turned. A small cumulus cloud and one or two bands of cirro-cumulus float peacefully by. It is a charming little study, but there is little in it to indicate the power of Palmer's later plates. But we are able to see in it the artist's close observation and accurate rendering of natural phenomena. The clouds, so often a stumbling block of artists, are accurately rendered and identifiable types. The shape of the tree is convincing, so much that one can sense the power of growth within it. The foliage, too, is brilliantly handled, and in those areas where the breeze is disturbing it one is reminded of the gentle movement observable in willows on any spring afternoon in the Fens or other areas where they abound. Yet this is no pollarded tree such as many are in those places. Here it is shown in its full majestic growth with all its natural potential realised. It has what Palmer himself called 'the grasp and grapple of the roots, the muscular belly and shoulders, the twisted sinews'.[1] Of the tree in the etching, A. H. Palmer wrote that it 'was practically copied from a careful water-colour study made from nature, and of a much larger size. Such a proceeding was very rare in any of Palmer's work. In this case, it may have been due, partly to a feeling of timidity in a new process, or, partly to a prudent wish not to endanger his election by anything too characteristic or ambitious'.[2]

In certain parts of the foliage, especially in the area just above the centre of the tree, the texture is faintly reminiscent of that to be seen on some of the Shoreham drawings, being realised in groups of little luminous dots.

The sky in 'The Willow' is represented in a conventional way, with parallel lines. We have already seen that Palmer was admonished for ruling some of them. He probably realised his error during work on the etching, for the lines lose their ruled regularity about a quarter of an inch from the top of the plate, at which point he began, with greater effect, to draw them freehand.

In 'The Willow' we are reminded of one of Palmer's beliefs – that 'a landscape, however lovely, was never perfect without at least some glint of water'.[3]

'The Willow' was the first of four plates etched in 1850. The next one, 'The Skylark' (Plate 2), shows what is a sudden flowering of a new visionary experience, a new discovery, through the medium of his etching, of the poetic quality which had eluded him since he left Shoreham. The opening of new visionary

---

[1] *Life and Letters*, p. 174. [2] *Victoria and Albert Museum Catalogue*, p. 56.
[3] Palmer, *Memoir*, p. 9.

vistas by a change of technique is not unknown. We have seen that Palmer was dissatisfied with water-colour, perhaps because he thought its possibilities were exhausted with the end of his period at Shoreham. He strove vainly to express himself in oils ; it was etching that gave him his outlet.

'The Skylark' showed considerable technical advance on 'The Willow', due to encouragement and instruction Palmer had received from Cope and Barlow. It is a simple scene. A man and his dog are coming through the gate of a cottage garden, the man looking up at a solitary skylark against a dawn sky with cirro-cumulus clouds. Of this sky, etched on a plate measuring only $4\frac{7}{8}$ by $4\frac{9}{16}$ inches, F. G. Stephens remarked : 'Light, searching through and through the cloud, has found nothing solid enough to reflect it, and therefore penetrates the body and is lost. The prodigious expanse of the atmosphere is thus represented in a way which is worthy of Turner himself.'[1] A cornfield, the garden of the cottage, distant hills, the nearer ones wooded, with a glimmer of water at their foot, are further elements in a scene that is flanked by trees at right and left. In the foreground, water, probably the edge of a pond, provides a touch of light.

The theme of 'The Skylark' fascinated Palmer for a long time. As early as 1831–2 he had painted a small sepia water-colour of the subject, almost the same composition as that of the etching, but showing the sky so early in the morning that stars still shone. Later he painted another version entitled 'The Rising of the Lark', a small panel picture. This was, wrote A. H. Palmer, 'begun before all hope of a return to oil painting was abandoned.'[2] It is said that Palmer's source was in Milton's *L'Allegro* :

> To hear the lark begin his flight,
> And singing startle the dull night,
> From his watch-towre in the skies,
> Till the dappled dawn doth rise.[3]

Palmer's next 1850 etching was 'The Herdsman's Cottage' or 'Sunset' (Plate 3). Like 'The Skylark' it has something of the Shoreham spirit in its conception. A herdsman, accompanied by his dog, is driving home his cattle through a woodland clearing, by a stream into which a spring is running. The herdsman's cottage is silhouetted at the left by the glare of the setting sun, the rays of which suffuse the whole composition and seem almost to dazzle. It is a peaceful scene of labour nearly completed.

---

[1] *Notes by Mr. F. G. Stephens on a Collection of Drawings, Paintings and Etchings by the late Samuel Palmer* (London, 1881) p. 15.

[2] *Life and Letters*, p. 74.

[3] Cf. Grigson, *op. cit.* p. 182. In 1927 the Cotswold Gallery, London, had an impression of this etching, inscribed by Palmer: 'To hear the lark begin his flight.'

Although it is a small work ($3\frac{13}{16}$ by 3 inches) 'The Herdsman's Cottage' is richly conceived. Deeply etched lines, especially on the farther bank of the brook and on the trunk of the large tree rising from it, are reminiscent of the thickly glued lines on some of the Shoreham drawings. The sun-rays, which could easily have been artificial in their impact, are completely convincing. The distant foliage, conceived in simple cross hatchings, has the right note of shadowy richness, like clouds in the sunset. The contrasted light and shade is magnificent. Here may be seen a realisation of Palmer's dictum: 'The ANIMATOR IS CHIAROSCURO. HOLES of DARK, BOLD CAST SHADOWS — the same PLAYFUL and INTRICATE sometimes, when cast from trees like (blueish) soft, cool gray, blotting or dappling over the finished matter (figures most beautiful under this effect). Where figures or sheep come in nearly front light against holes of shade under trees they are like plates or bassi-relievi of wrought gold.'[1]

In 1872, twenty-two years after its creation, 'The Herdsman's Cottage' was published in *The Portfolio* with the erroneous title 'Sunrise'. There had been long drawn out negotiations for the sale of the plate between Palmer and Hamerton, who acted on behalf of the publishers of *The Portfolio*, Seeley and Co. At first Palmer was reluctant to name a price, but at last said he wanted thirty-five guineas. Hamerton replied: 'Seeley though a prudent publisher is by no means a niggardly one and does not hesitate in paying in quite a princely fashion when he can make it answer to do so. It seems you want 35 gs, for you little plate. If we went by our tastes and feelings we should give it without hesitation, but as things are Seeley would do better, I think, to wait a bit. . . .'[2] Some time after this Hamerton offered £25 to Palmer for the outright purchase of a plate – £5 more than the usual amount paid. There was, however, a condition – that Palmer should start work on it and keep it by him 'for some months till it seemed to have grown into a condition of sufficiently developed beauty'.[3] This offer – an extra £5 for months of working on a new plate to bring it to the desired level of refinement – did not tempt Palmer, since it was little more than he could obtain for one proof of some of his etchings. He therefore refused. In the end he did sell the plate of 'The Herdsman's Cottage' to Seeley's, and the price was so adjusted that in addition to a cash payment he received a number of proofs.

The last of the 1850 etchings was 'Christmas' or 'Folding the Last Sheep' (Plate 4). It is about the same size as 'The Skylark' and 'The Herdsman's Cottage', measuring $3\frac{7}{8}$ by $3\frac{3}{16}$ inches. Its theme is taken from a sonnet by John Codrington Bampfield:[4]

> With footstep slow, in furry pall yclad,
> His brows enwreathed with holly never sere,

[1] *Life and Letters*, p. 82.   [2] *Victoria and Albert Museum Catalogue*, p. 74.   [3] *ibid.*   [4] 1754–96.

Old Christmas comes to close the wanèd year,
And aye the shepherd's heart to make right glad ;
Who, when his teeming flocks are homeward had,
To blazing hearth repairs, and nut-brown beer ;
And views well pleased the ruddy prattlers dear
Hug the grey mongrel ; meanwhile maid and lad
Squabble for roasted crabs. Thee, sire, we hail,
Whether thine aged limbs thou dost enshroud
In vest of snowy white and hoary veil,
Or wrapp'st thy visage in a sable cloud ;
Thee we proclaim with mirth and cheer, nor fail
To greet thee well, with many a carol loud.

A full moon sails in the sky behind bare deciduous trees ; elsewhere there are evergreens. The cottage stands at the left, with the shepherd's wife inside laying the table for supper. She may be seen through the open door in a cosy light. A little boy, a girl and a smaller child have rushed out to greet the shepherd, their father, and his dog. The shepherd is with one hand closing the fold on the last of his sheep ; with the other he holds the hand of his youngest child. The gleam of water is provided by a puddle in the left foreground. It is a scene in which we may see Palmer trying 'for the primitive cottage feeling' that he wrote about in his sketchbook.[1]

The composition of 'Christmas' is in many ways reminiscent of illustration No. XVII in Blake's *Virgil* wood engravings (Plate 30) and I think it is likely that we can here see the influence of that work on Palmer. The pose of Palmer's shepherd as he folds his last sheep is not unlike that of Blake's elder shepherd as he takes his younger companion's sheep to fold with his own :

This might they care with me forget, and fold
Thy flock with mine, to ward th' injurious cold.

Blake's work, too, has a cottage in the composition with a sheep-pen adjoining, though the positions are different from those in the etching. Yet another figure in the Blake *Virgil* engravings that is reminiscent of Palmer's shepherd is the left-hand figure in illustration No. V (Plate 29).

On the plate for 'Christmas', A. H. Palmer made his first essays in retroussage under Goulding's tuition. 'We had got over the first stages of the printer's art very quickly. . . . It now came to a matter of "hands" ; and, more especially, to those very things which my father had been endeavouring to teach me for years. In the first

---

[1] 1824 Sketchbook, p. III.

case, entomology had taught me lightness of touch beyond anything needed in printing. Goulding printed a proof showing the full benefits of what he then called *retroussage*, and cleaned the margin. He then stood back and said nothing more. His teaching had been so absolutely clear all along, so admirably worded, and so kind, that I practically reproduced his proof. This was the foundation laid on which my father at once began to build; the troubles of nearly a quarter of a century were over.'[1]

Palmer's next etching – 'The Vine' or 'Plumpy Bacchus' – was published in 1852 (Plate 5). It consists of two subjects on one plate, illustrating these lines from Shakespeare's *Antony and Cleopatra*:

> Come thou monarch of the Vine
> Plumpy Bacchus with pink eyne:
> In thy vats our cares be drown'd;
> In thy grapes our hairs be crown'd;
> Cup us till the world go round;
> Cup us till the world go round![2]

The mood of this etching is entirely different from those we have so far discussed. It is essentially classical. The upper subject shows devotees taking part in a bacchanalian scene, abandoning themselves to pleasure while grapes drop from the baskets in which they have been gathered. Two of the devotees have seen their god, resplendent in light, running towards them, and they hold out their hands in ecstatic greeting. In the lower subject putti collect rich bunches of grapes from a vine entwined around a massive tree. Here again we may perhaps see the influence of one of Palmer's friends – Calvert, whose 'Cyder Feast' (Plate 31) is conceived in the same spirit of hedonist abandon. Twenty-four years separated the creation of the two works, but as we have seen, Palmer kept Calvert's engravings as 'mind toners'. Certain details seem also to be closely related. The primitive ladders leaning against the trees in each composition, though in reversed positions, are almost exactly alike. The god running down the slope in the upper subject of the etching has something in common with the main figures in Calvert's work. Upset baskets of fruit, symbolising abundance, appear in each.

The handling of the plate of 'The Vine' is fine, but it lacks something of the richness of the work in 'The Skylark', 'Christmas' and 'The Herdsman's Cottage'. It is a more trivial work than any of those, but it still has a certain power while lacking their visionary insight. The etching was published in 1853 as one of the works in *Songs and Ballads of Shakespeare illustrated by the Etching Club*.

Palmer's next etching was not published until 1857, five years after the appear-

---

[1] *Victoria and Albert Museum Catalogue*, pp. 75–6.   [2] Act II, Scene 7.

ance of 'The Vine'. It is 'The Sleeping Shepherd; Early Morning' (Plate 6). Its mood is pastoral, a return to that of the 1850 etchings and in particular that of 'The Skylark'. As in that work the time represented is at about dawn, but it is a little later, the light is softer and the air more vaporous. Beneath a trellised vine, leaning on a bale of straw against a cottage wall, sleeps the shepherd. Beside him is his crook and a small bound book. Beyond him are folded sheep, closely related in appearance to the sheep in the Shoreham drawings. Farther still into the background are trees and bushes, distinguishable among which is, to the right, a sturdy hawthorn tree. Behind these a gentle slope rises against the sky, and ascending it are the silhouetted forms of a ploughman and his oxen. The sky is peaceful, with a little sparse cloud reflected in the light of the rising sun. Rooks rise in a curve which reaches from the sheep to above the ploughman and his team, and serve as an adroit device to consolidate the composition.

Among Palmer's etchings this is his nearest approach to the Shoreham spirit and expression. I have mentioned the closeness of the sheep to his early drawings. The handling of the distant foliage, too, is reminiscent of it, in particular that of the hawthorn. This handling evokes Palmer's own words, written in his sketchbook. 'These trees brilliantly lighted up by ye rising sun those parts brightest against the line of the field which was in shadow but white with frosty dew . . . Note perhaps at sunrise the light makes more massy lumps of brightness than the sunset.'[1] And is the little book at the shepherd's side a reminder of that other little volume of Milton published by Jacob Tonson, which Mary Ward had given to Palmer? Writing to Valpy in June 1864 Palmer recalled that he had carried this in his pocket for twenty years.[2] It was in a 'smooth and rounded brass and darkly polished leather binding',[3] which could also be a description of the one in the etching. The possible association is more strongly suggested by these lines from *L'Allegro*, which seem in places to fit the scene portrayed in the etching :

> The Plowman neer at hand,
> Whistles o'er the Furrow'd Land,
> And the Milkmaid singeth blithe,
> And the Mower whets his sithe,
> And every Shepherd tells his tale
> Under the Hawthorn in the dale.

Like 'The Skylark', 'The Sleeping Shepherd' had a precursor in Palmer's earlier paintings. In this case the setting is slightly different, but the figure of the Shepherd himself is almost exactly the same as that in the etching, but in reverse (Frontispiece). The figure was probably derived from a Graeco-Roman figure in the British

[1] 1824 Sketchbook, p. 89.   [2] *Life and Letters*, p. 255.   [3] *Palmer Memoir*, p. 7.

Museum – 'Endymion the Shepherd Boy asleep on Mt. Latmos' (Plate 33), though Palmer mistook the figure for Mercury. He mentioned it in a letter to Valpy, in September 1864 : 'Below, in the Townley Gallery, is the sure test of our imaginative faculty – the sleeping Mercury. More than two thousand years ago the sculptor bade that marble live. It lived, but slept, and it is living still. Bend over it. Look at those delicate eyelids ; that mouth a little open. He is dreaming. Dream on, marble shepherd ; few will disturb your slumber.'[1] He had mentioned the work earlier, in 1834, in a letter to Richmond, writing of its 'hard-to-be-defined but most delicious quality to perfection'.[2]

We know that Palmer in his youth copied antique statues and he carried memories of them into his middle and later years. About 1823 – 4 he had written of his 'attempts to copy the Antique statues to try and draw most severely, and to cry out for more and more form ; and then I shall find in the Antique more than I can copy, if I look and look and pry into it earnestly for form. I shall not be easy till I have drawn one Antique statue *most severely*'.[3]

Another etching published by Palmer in 1857 is 'The Rising Moon' or 'An English Pastoral' (Plate 7). It is larger than any of the previous subjects ($4\frac{19}{32}$ by $7\frac{1}{2}$ inches). Elements from Palmer's Shoreham period, from his visits to Devon and from his Italian honeymoon may be discerned in it.

A shepherd, with a stick and bundle over his shoulder, stands with his flock on a slope overlooking a village in a valley. The figure is like many of those to be found in pictures of the Shoreham period, in particular the one in the water-colour/gouache drawing 'Cornfield by Moonlight, with the Evening Star' (Plate 34), though in that the shepherd is walking with his stick instead of carrying it. At the right-hand side of the etching, in front of the shepherd and some of his sheep is a provender trough. A small tree, probably a hawthorn, stands at the left-hand side. Behind the village is a hill, and the moon is rising from behind its right-hand slope, illuminating the church tower and the village roofs. Illumination also comes from one or two windows and from the reflected light in a pool behind the hawthorn. Light cirrus clouds reach from side to side of the sky. To the right of, and slightly in front of the village is a group of trees, including cypresses. These recall Palmer's drawings of those at the Villa d'Este (Plate 21). The sea, dark and indistinct, reaches away into the distance at the right.

During May 1858, Palmer began work on 'The Weary Ploughman', originally known as 'The Herdsman ; or Tardus Bubulcus' (Plate 8). It took him six weeks to etch. This large plate – the etched surface measures $5\frac{3}{16}$ by $7\frac{15}{16}$ inches – marks the beginning of Palmer's finest etched work.

[1] *Life and Letters*, p. 261.

[2] *ibid.* p. 183. A figure somewhat reminiscent of that in 'The Sleeping Shepherd' is on page 107 of the 1824 Sketchbook.

[3] *Life and Letters*, p. 13.

F

S.P.E.

By the light of the rising moon a man is returning home driving a pair of cattle before him; a calf walks beside him. Like the shepherd in 'The Rising Moon' he carries a pole, but with a basket suspended from it. To his left is a horse-chestnut tree in blossom and to his right a large barberry bush sprawls away from him with many little shoots growing around it. As in 'The Rising Moon' a village nestles in the valley, but here it is a village of thatched cottages and buildings, rather more rustic than those in the earlier etching. One or two windows show light. Hills like Devonshire tors rise in the distance. A waterfall may be seen glittering from among the trees on one of the slopes. The crest of the hill at the right is surmounted with pine trees. The sky is a *tour de force* and recalls the work of Turner. The great disc of the full moon, the cirrus threads, and the stars at the top right-hand corner, make an impressive background.

According to A. H. Palmer, 'The Ploughman going home' and 'Tardus Bubulcus' are the original names of the work. The title 'The Herdsman', he claimed, was nonsense.[1] But it is, to say the least, unlikely that ploughing would have been in progress in May when the horse-chestnut was in blossom. One would expect, too, to see some other evidence that the oxen had been ploughing; perhaps they would be shown as described by the Rev. Francis Kilvert in his diary: '. . . I fell in with a team of red oxen, harnessed, coming home from plough with chains rattling and the old ploughman riding the fore ox. . . .'[2] It may, therefore, be that 'The Herdsman' after all is the right title. The presence of the calf might be additional evidence for it, for it would hardly have been needed during ploughing.

Palmer used a graver in places on this plate, giving the impressions a rich lustre with thick lines such as we have already noticed. This, and other details of his procedures of technique are described by Palmer himself in the following notes.

First biting in June 1. hour; with one part of Nitrous acid to $4\frac{1}{2}$ of water. Hot weather, but no artificial heat used. In the sky, only the darkest bars of cloud and darker masses of cloud and azure — deep azure of moonlight were etched. All the sky stopped out. Great care used to do so neatly against distant hills and leaves of tree. Stopped out high lights on the backs of cattle and all the figure except extreme darks between folds of drapery . . . removed, split, or narrowed with Brunswick black[3] lines which were bitten too broad for their place, or were likely to embarrass. Removed, split, dotted or narrowed intersections of lines likely to become spots. S.O.[4] the highest light in foreground.

---

[1] *Victoria and Albert Museum Catalogue*, p. 78.
[2] *Kilvert's Diary 1870–1879*. Edited by William Plomer. London (1967) p. 260.
[3] Brunswick black is a black varnish, similar to black Japan.
[4] i.e. Stopped out.

Second biting about one hour . . . Stopped or dotted the deepest bitings in the distance. S.O. the smoke in cottage. Stopped over the broad lights on cattle. Stopped the figure wholly, and went over the whole, stopping, painting, dotting, or splitting the widening lines . . .

I think we may be free to use close hatching and repeated cross hatchings with the NEEDLE if very careful with the partial STOPPINGS.

Third biting, June 21st $1\frac{1}{2}$ hours – Mr. Barlow says that George Cook said that FIVE MINUTES of careful stoppings out, were worth a Day's Work on the etching itself.

June 22 began by minutely stopping out the now numerous places in the distance where the lines had bitten broad enough . . . stopped out round the figure a little beyond the outline. I also continued broken shadows strongly with the needle and in deep shadows split or mended parts which were biting too broadly. 22nd June. Increased strength of acid from $4\frac{1}{2}$ to 1 acid, to 4 water to 1 acid. Fourth Biting, $\frac{1}{4}$ hour. S.O. hundreds of particles . . . 23rd June. 5th Biting, $\frac{1}{4}$ hour. Then stopped out whole of cattle &c., so the darkest parts of the cattle were bitten 4 hours. By this time nearly the whole of the distance was stopped. 6th Biting $\frac{1}{4}$ hour, making the deepest shadows under the chestnut tree, and the darkest lines of shadow in near tree trunk $4\frac{1}{2}$ hours.

A new light bursts upon me! Let me have always a wiped and an unwiped proof and work from unwiped impressions – except in the focuses. Thus the work may have more of the vigour and texture of old woodcuts and the plate will be less worn . . . I then did a good deal with the graver, but left the sky, and on July 3. (1858) Mr. Gad took 4 proofs . . . Also two other proofs not wiped at all, or as he calls it wiped to the canvas; i.e. as far as the canvas wiping but not as far as the muslin wiping; and another wiped to the muslin, this last I think is a most excellent way of printing – acting on the etching as a glazing on the prepared picture and I think it will save a great deal of work, add mystery, and be my best plan for the future.[1]

'The Weary Ploughman' is a fine plate. But the one that followed in 1861, after an interval of three years, is even finer. This is 'The Early Ploughman' (Plate 9), originally known by the longer title of 'The Morning Spread upon the Mountains'.

At sunrise a ploughman is driving his team of oxen over a small field beside a bridged stream. A second ploughman with another team of oxen is working in the distance. The nearer one is watched by a woman standing before a group of cypresses. On her head she carries a pitcher and in her left hand is another container. Beyond the stream at the left a hill rises with ruins on its slope. In the distance are hills, probably a memory of Italian alps, against a sky that is similar

[1] *Victoria & Albert Museum Catalogue*, pp. 76–8.

to that in 'The Weary Ploughman', but seen at sunrise. Peewits fly over the left-hand side of the composition, helping to tie the composition together; they are assisted in this by the tree which grows below them.

Some elements in this etching may be found in Palmer's earlier tempera/oil painting 'The Shearers' (*circa* 1833–4) (Plate 35). The attitude of the ploughman in the etching, for instance, closely resembles, in reverse, that of the central figure in the group of sheep-shearers, aptly described by Mr. Sacheverell Sitwell as 'The shepherd kings, or the kings of the golden corn'.[1] The ploughman's hat, too, is similar to the straw hat hanging with a scythe and other implements in the barn entrance in the painting. Palmer sometimes wore such a hat himself. The group of cypresses is again derived from the study of those at the Villa d'Este (Plate 21).[2] The figures of the ploughman and his oxen, and some other details in the etching, also closely resemble those in the illustration to 'Lycidas' in *The Minor Poems of John Milton*.

It is, however, the little figure of the woman that opens up the most intriguing possibilities. It is close in feeling and in its expression to the small figure at the left-hand side of Calvert's wood engraving 'The Brook' (Plate 32). That figure was probably derived from one in a water-colour by Blake, 'Jacob's Ladder' (Plate 36),[3] and Palmer's figure is reminiscent of the one second from the left in the same work. Each of these figures – Blake's, Calvert's and Palmer's – has relationships with similar figures found on Greek and Roman gems and coins, and it is a fact that all three artists were interested in these little works of art. We have Palmer's own authority for Blake's interest in them, in a letter he wrote to Gilchrist: 'When he approached . . . some of the inventions preserved in the Antique Gems, all his powers were concentrated in admiration.'[4] Calvert's work is full of their influence.[5] Palmer had a collection of plaster casts from antique gems[6] and some miniature antique busts which he kept in wooden boxes or calico bags.[7] He referred to these in a letter to a Miss Wilkinson, written on 29 May 1862: 'Mr. Newman made me eight or ten of his cedar colour-boxes without partitions, and a little deeper than usual, in which I possess a fine sculpture-gallery, having filled them with casts from the finest antique gems. These are most useful for reference, when working out lines caught from nature. I assure you there is nothing far-fetched in this. All the best landscape-painters have studied figures a great deal. Mr. Rogers used to prize a Claude of his the more because the figure was painted by Claude himself. I would advise you to collect casts from the best antique gems whenever you can get them.'[8]

[1] *Narrative Pictures* (London, 1937) p. 63.   [2] Cf. Hardie, Martin, *Samuel Palmer* (London, 1928) p. 13.
[3] Lister, *Edward Calvert*, p. 84.
[4] Gilchrist, Alexander, *Life of William Blake* (London, 1880) Vol. I, p. 346.
[5] Lister, *Edward Calvert*, pp. 62, 72, 84, 89 and *passim*.   [6] *Life and Letters*, p. 147 f.n.
[7] *ibid.* p. 144.   [8] *ibid.* p. 236.

There we have proof in Palmer's own words that he had antique gems much in mind about the time he was working on 'The Early Ploughman', and it is probable that the little female figure in that work was inspired by some such old gem.[1]

Palmer commenced work on another etching about 1860–1. This is 'The Morning of Life' (Plate 10); in some ways it is close in feeling to the upper subject in 'The Vine'. It has been variously named 'Hercules and Cacus', 'Sheep-washing', 'A Leafy Dell' and 'The Morning of Life'. Of its original state as 'Hercules and Cacus', Palmer wrote to Hamerton on 26 January 1872: '. . . . it was begun years ago to illustrate a classical subject; but finding that I could no-how clip my poodle into lion-shape, I even let the hair grow, and christened him for the Art Union, *The Morning of Life*.'[2]

This refers to the publication of the latest state of the etching in *Etchings for the Art-Union of London by the Etching Club* (1872).[3] For this five hundred and forty poor impressions were printed. 'Fifteen were sent to the loathing etcher – fifteen slaps in the face.'[4] They were printed by Goulding, which is surprising when we consider his reputation. But although he blamed the poor impressions on to the poor pay he received, it was probably due as much to his inexperience, for he was, as A. H. Palmer put it, 'not yet the glorious creature of Shepherd's Bush Road.'[5]

The scene is set in a woodland clearing with the rays of the rising sun spreading through the trees. In a stream at the right-hand side men are washing sheep. In the centre of the composition a kneeling woman[6] is gathering fallen apples and placing them in a basket. Another man, standing in the stream and leaning against the bank, is talking to her. At the left two boys are hauling a sheep across the clearing so that it may be washed in its turn. It is a scene, seemingly far removed from its original subject, the pursuit of a cattle-stealer by Hercules.

This etching was followed seven years later, in 1879, by Palmer's two greatest plates, 'The Bellman' and 'The Lonely Tower' (Plates 11 and 12), both inspired by these lines from Milton's *Il Penseroso*:

> – the Belman's drowsie charm,
> To bless the dores from nightly harm :
> Or let my Lamp at midnight hour,
> Be seen in some high lonely Towr,
> Where I may oft out-watch the *Bear*,
> With thrice-great *Hermes*. . . .

[1] Cf. for example Plate 23. This is taken from Plate LXXVII of King, C. W., *Handbook of Engraved Gems*, Second Edition (London, 1885).
[2] *Life and Letters*, p. 323.
[3] See Catalogue of the Etchings, p. 106.   [4] *Victoria and Albert Museum Catalogue*, p. 81.
[5] *Victoria and Albert Museum Catalogue*, p. 80.   [6] This figure was originally that of Hercules.

Each is a large plate, easily the biggest in Palmer's *œuvre*. The measurements of 'The Bellman' are $6\frac{9}{16}$ by $9\frac{3}{16}$ inches, and of 'The Lonely Tower', $6\frac{1}{2}$ by $9\frac{3}{16}$ inches.

In 'The Bellman' we again have a village in a valley. This time it really is Shoreham, though its surrounding countryside is imaginative. 'It is,' wrote Palmer to Hamerton on 4 August 1879, 'a breaking out of village-fever long after contact – a dream of that genuine village where I mused away some of my best years, designing what nobody would care for, and contracting, among good books, a fastidious and unpopular taste. I had no room in my *Bellman* for that translucent current, rich with trout, a river not unknown to song;[1] nor for the so-called "idiot" on the bridge with whom I always chatted – like to like perhaps. But there were all the village appurtenances – the wise-woman behind the age, still resorted to; the shoemaker always before it, such virtue is in the smell of leather; the rumbling mill, and haunted mansion[2] in a shadowy paddock, where sceptics had seen more than they could account for; the vicarage with its learned traditions; and Wordsworth brought to memory every three hours, by

> "– the crazy old church clock
> And the bewilder'd chimes."

Byron would have stuffed his ears with cotton had he been forced to live there.'[3]

Just entering this village with its twinkling lights, walks the bellman ringing his bell. A couple sitting in a bower at the left glance at him as he passes, and at the right cattle are lying, among them a young calf. Behind the houses at the left is a horse-chestnut in blossom, and in the distance rise tor-like hills. The moon, a great disc, is ascending over them among cirrus clouds.

We have it on the authority of A. H. Palmer that the plate for 'The Bellman' received thirteen bitings, with much stopping out between them. 'After the first biting, the needle work was nearly doubled, and more was added after the second, third and seventh. The plate was proved by me at our press and was finished without catastrophe.'[4]

'The Lonely Tower' is a powerful work. It is moonlight and the horned waning moon is low in the sky with the constellations of The Great Bear and the Heavenly Twins twinkling above; there are a few light clouds. On a tor stands a tower[5] with a light shining through one of its window apertures. A lonely traveller on the left of the hill is climbing towards it. The foreground is cleft by a deep chasm at

[1] The Darent.

[2] Cf. Lister, *Edward Calvert*, pp. 29–30. Wrongly described there as Shoreham Castle; it was really Shoreham Place. Communicated by Mr. C. Franklin White.

[3] *Life and Letters*, pp. 377–8.　　　　[4] *Victoria and Albert Museum Catalogue*, p. 83.

[5] The tower is thought by some to have been inspired by that at Lee Abbey, Lynton, Devon. I am indebted to Mr. Edward Malins for this information.

the bottom of which flows a river. On the left of this, protected by a stone wall, is a road, along which a waggoner leads his team. A figure, apparently asleep, is riding within. On the right of the chasm some sheep are taking their rest beneath hawthorn trees. In the foreground is a provender trough and just behind it two shepherds lie and gaze up at the light in the tower. An owl flies along the chasm. On the skyline immediately in front of the moon is a row of 'druidic' trilithons.

It is a scene of deep feeling. A sense of nostalgia pervades it. The two shepherds for instance, are looking towards the light in the tower as if they are longing for something that they cannot approach because of the chasm between. On the other side of the chasm one small figure is attempting to reach it on foot, another is being conveyed there in a wagon. The sheep rest safely despite the yawning cleft nearby. The trilithons on the horizon remind us that the powers of darkness are ever present, waiting to ensnare the unwary. This is a symbol Palmer probably took from Blake, to whom the Druids and their temples symbolised natural religion.[1] The waning moon adds to the feeling of nostalgia. It is as if its light has illumined a landscape symbolising man's everlasting spiritual struggle, his longing and striving by various means to attain the lonely tower of spiritual grace, while the pitfalls of false religion and the chasm of nonentity are ever present, ready to entrap him.

'The Lonely Tower' received fourteen bitings and much stopping out. It was published in *Il Penseroso* for the Etching Club by R. Ansdell in 1880, but the result failed to please Palmer, who wrote: 'So the dear old Etching Club revives on the 15th. – I love it though it has quite smashed me by the way my *Lonely Tower* has been printed. Full directions were sent to the printer, and a model proof, but in vain.'[2]

Some claim that 'The Early Ploughman' is Palmer's finest etching.[3] It is indeed a fine work, but I feel that for true nobility of conception and realisation 'The Bellman' and especially 'The Lonely Tower' are finer. The deeply etched lines of the latter give full effect to Palmer's love for thick, rich, raised lines. The symbolism of these etchings is confident, their detail based on an accurate observation of nature. If we are to see in Palmer's etchings a return to visionary work, it is here above all.

Palmer's next completed etching, begun in 1880, was 'Opening the Fold' or 'Early Morning', an illustration to the following lines in the Eighth Eclogue of Virgil in Palmer's translation:

---

[1] For the sake of accuracy it should be noted that such trilithons as those in this etching are now thought to have been nothing to do with the Druids. They are almost certainly the remains of megalithic tombs. But to Blake they were druidic.

[2] Ivimy MSS.; *Victoria and Albert Museum Catalogue*, pp. 83–4.

[3] Mr. James Laver once wrote that Palmer never did anything better than 'The Sleeping Shepherd', *A History of Etching* (London, 1929) p. 113. Opinions in such matters will always differ.

Scarce with her rosy fingers had the dawn
From glimmering heaven the veil of night withdrawn,
And folded flocks were loose to browse anew
O'er mountain thyme or trefoil wet with dew,
When leaning sad an olive stem beside,
These, his last numbers, hapless Damon plied.

It is dawn and a few stars remain in the sky. A shepherd unfolds his sheep while his companion, leaning against a tree, pipes a melody. A provender trough is in the foreground. Behind the sheepfold is a thatched cottage with smoke rising from its chimney. The landscape is divided by a lush valley through which a river flows. A town lies in the distance, and beyond it is a range of craggy alpine hills. Rooks circle in the sky, and rays of sunshine strike through wisps of cloud. It is a pastoral par excellence, compared by Mr. Sacheverell Sitwell to Handel's 'My heart ever faithful' and 'The sheep may safely graze'.[1]

The story of the inception of this work is interesting. According to his son, Palmer 'was now intellectually vigorous, and entirely free from all but the normal infirmity of a sedentary man of his age. . . . He seemed to have escaped unusually well the effects of old age on the judgement and manipulative dexterity. Having completed twelve plates in about thirty years, he, now, at the age of seventy-four, deliberately made preparations and bought the plates for ten more. . . . The first of the intended ten is known as *Early Morning*, or *Opening The Fold*. . . . The bitings began on the 16th of August 1880, and were eleven in number before the first proof was taken.'[2]

To Hamerton, 'Opening The Fold' was 'the most completely beautiful of all Samuel Palmer's etchings. . . . It is full of air and space, the eye wanders over it for miles, and yet at the same time there is a sweet solemnity in it. . . . My own first impression was wonder that a man of Palmer's age should have been able to execute such a piece of work. To say that there is no trace of decadence in that plate would be true but not true enough. The plate is the perfect consummation of Palmer's experience, knowledge, and manual power.'[3]

'Opening The Fold' was the main subject of a letter written by Palmer on 22 October 1880 to his son:

Dear Herbert, However much tempests may rage before and after the Hours of ART-WORK MUST BE QUIET HOURS, and printing like yours *is* art work. When we want a Lambent flame we clear the grate, getting the noise & dust over *for the time*.

[1] *Splendours and Miseries* (London, 1943) p. 186.   [2] *Victoria and Albert Museum Catalogue*, p. 85.
[3] *ibid.*

[88]

If anything bustles me, I am forced to sit still & make an artificial quiet, before I can put a right touch.

Success in the printing of this etching – which printing is your interest as well as mine, depends on delight in solitude & locked doors, a contemplative mood & intense concentration. Indeed these are the conditions of all high excellence.

Men who have these enjoy society all the more by contrast. However much torn by business outside, the great men have been quiet in their studios . . . I confess that when I get out of my little charmed circle of quiet I am horribly flustered – just a time of life too when I want repose of mind . . .

I have just opened the 2 proofs – Pray throw your brown ink into the dust-hole. I have sometimes thought that, in punishment perhaps for some long forgotten sins – a malignant demon has been suffered to dash the cup from my lip – just when I thought some peculiar benefit had mercifully been sent. Such a demon could have done no worse than to suggest 'brown ink' to you. Both this and the former brown one, are, (to adopt a critical phrase of Horsley's[1]) 'BEASTLY'.

The Black impression is so very good (the sky absolutely *perfect*) that ten minutes work upon the plate would be enough. – The success of this etching may hasten the realization of your domestic hopes – If it sells off at once, I will D.V. as soon as possible, do another as companion, the same size – · · · (on the same money arrangement with you) – to keep the success going – thus profitably filling up your time when not otherwise engaged.

But, as this little etching *may* be *a turning point* I say again consider of *your* kind of printing (as Sir Joshua says to the painter) that you must always stand with the BALANCES IN YOUR HAND, that Whoever balances must attend, – whoever attends, must, during that mental operation '*be quiet*' . . .

The edge of the tree A[2] is at the top a trifle too light and may be amended by two lines like mine in the Red Chalk.

2ndly The sucking lamb's bended knee is slightly too light at the joint, & a very little too long perhaps, which rather injures the perspicuity of the action.

3 Perhaps the *lower* part of the clump of trees BB[3] – is wiped rather too hard.

4 As to general effect I have to suggest only that the darkest parts of the bushes behind figure should be the deepest dark in the subject & a little darker than the cool dip into the river-reeks – between the figure opening the fold and the great pine stem – which is quite light enough pray do not use the match either there or on the river lights.

The essence of this etching is *crispness* – and anything like the tint left by too thin an ink between the lines, fatal –

[1] William Horsley, an original member of the 'Old' Etching Club.

[2] This is the Scots pine at the extreme left-hand side, to the left of the two small figures who are looking towards the distant city. Palmer has drawn a sketch in his letter to identify it.

[3] This is the clump of trees behind the Scots pine A.

5 Perhaps the dark side of the provender trough is too hard wiped.

I hope you will go over the above carefully as it has cost me my best daylight.

When you have availed yourself of the 5 foregoing suggestions it will be sufficient I think to send me one more proof but no more Browns. Oh – no more Browns . . .[1]

I have never seen a Palmer etching printed in brown ink. In view of Palmer's violent reaction to the colour in this letter, we may assume that any so printed would have been destroyed.

When he died Palmer had begun work on four more plates to illustrate his translation of Virgil. As we have seen, they were completed by his son. No details have been handed down to us of the extent of the work of each etcher on these plates. They are 'The Homeward Star' (Plate 14), 'The Cypress Grove' (Plate 15), 'The Sepulchre' (Plate 16), and 'Moeris and Galatea' (Plate 17). Of these the first is close to the Shoreham sentiment. The remainder are more closely related to 'The Vine'. It would be dangerous to hazard a guess as to which contains most of the father's work, but I have the feeling that 'The Homeward Star' is closer to him both in handling and conception. It is in any case the most attractive of the four. Two cottagers, after a hard day's work, are eating a simple meal in the open air beneath the waxing moon and evening star. A woman is offering them apples. Cattle and goats and trees laden with fruit give an air of abundance. A thatched cottage nestles at the foot of a hill and above it birds are flying home to roost. Farther up the side of the hill is a small town. A waterfall splashes down the central slope and in the distance are crags.

'The Cypress Grove' is a pretty starlit classical scene illustrating the lines :

> Untimely lost, and by a cruel death,
> The Nymphs their Daphnis mourn'd with faltering breath.
> O bowers of hazel, waters murmuring hoarse,
> Ye heard that mother's cry : she, the dear corse
> Embracing in a long, a last caress,
> Planets and gods rebuked as pitiless.

The form and growth of the cypress trees which give the grove its name are reminiscent of those of the Monterey cypress (*Cupressus macrocarpa*) which, though pyramidal when young, become wide-spreading with maturity. If this is the species represented it is somewhat strange to see it in a Greek scene, for it is a native of California.

[1] Ivimy MSS.

'The Sepulchre' is a scene of witchcraft by the setting moon. It has some dramatic power :

> And while the troubled moon shrunk in and set,
> Th'earth trembled, and the starless heaven was jet,
> With such as I am crumbling in my hand,
> Could he the sad and shadowy past command
> At will, and while my senses crept with dread,
> From a deep sepulchre call up the dead.

'Moeris and Galatea' is the least successful of the group ; it is a muddled composition in which the various elements fail to cohere. I cannot help thinking that there is very little of Samuel Palmer's work in it. It illustrates the lines :

> Then, to our goats at milking time return
> O'er breezy heather-bells and slopes of vine ;
> The cream-bowl set and in our cave recline,
> (Its brows with poplar shaded, watch the West),
> And timely, with the sun, together rest.

This group of etchings is certainly of considerable interest. But we must not be tempted to judge Palmer by them, since the extent of his work here is uncertain. His own etched work ended with the completion of the masterly 'Opening the Fold'. Nine weeks before his death, with his Virgil plates at hand, he wrote to his son these words : 'The painter's and the poet's struggles are solitary and patient ; silent and sublime. "I tremble when I sit down to paint a flower", said W. Hunt.'[1] Here, in his etchings, we may observe Palmer at work, not in the intensity of his Valley of Vision, surrounded by his fellow 'Ancients', not in the tameness of his subsequent paintings, but 'solitary and patient ; silent and sublime' in his favourite medium. Well might he have spoken the lines, if he had known them, of the poet William Butler Yeats, who was, in our own century, to be much influenced by him :

> Picture and book remain,
> An acre of green grass
> For air and exercise,
> Now strength of body goes ;
> Midnight, an old house
> Where nothing stirs but a mouse.

[1] *Victoria and Albert Museum Catalogue*, p. 87.

My temptation is quiet.
Here at life's end
Neither loose imagination,
Nor the mill of the mind
Consuming its rag and bone,
Can make the truth known.

Grant me an old man's frenzy,
Myself must I remake
Till I am Timon and Lear
Or that William Blake
Who beat upon the wall
Till Truth obeyed his call;

A mind Michael Angelo knew
That can pierce the clouds,
Or inspired by frenzy
Shake the dead in their shrouds;
Forgotten else by mankind,
An old man's eagle mind.[1]

[1] 'An Acre of Grass' from *Last Poems* (1936–9).

IV

Legacies

The posthumous influence of Samuel Palmer's etchings has not been as great as that of his Shoreham work, yet it is important notwithstanding. It is found both in the visual arts and in literature.

Palmer's etching enlarged the bounds of the art and it was therefore natural that it should have had some impact on later work. At first his work was seen by some as 'false etching'. We have already noted P. G. Hamerton's view that Palmer was 'less a true etcher than a noble painter expressing himself with the etching-needle' (p. 74). Let us return to the passage, which I will now quote in full.

Etchers may be divided broadly into two classes ; the true etchers who show the etched line frankly, and rely upon it, and make the most of it, such as Rembrandt, Vandyke, Whistler, and Haden ; and the false etchers, who, though they may be exquisite artists, do not understand the value of the naked line, but hide it under more or less successful imitations of brush-work or burin-work. When this book was first projected, it was resolved to exclude the false etchers altogether, but on further investigation, it became evident that such severity would compel the writer to pass in silence almost all modern English work ; it was finally decided to speak of the false etchers with the kind of respect which is due to them, a respect in many cases amounting to veneration for noble artistic qualities, though limited on technical grounds by the falsity of their method.

In using the word 'false' in this purely technical sense, let me not be understood to imply that there is any defect of truth or sincerity in the artistic interpretation of nature. Samuel Palmer is a false etcher, in this technical sense, but he is one of the truest, most sincere, most richly-gifted artists who ever used water-colour, and his etchings themselves are amongst the most exquisite and admirable works of art ever wrought in England. Works of art! at a time when, amongst the enormous production of painted canvases and etched or engraved coppers going on in Europe, works of art are yet by no means of frequent occurrence.

The aim of Samuel Palmer as an executant, is a certain richness and tenderness always subordinated to feeling. It never runs away with him, but pauses for the varying thought. His etchings are pure poetry, every gleam and hint in them is due to some sweet ineffable sentiment. I never spoke to him and do not praise his

[93]

work from any personal interest in its author ; but during the negotiations about the plate which is given herewith,[1] he wrote to me one or two letters, and asked amongst other things if I had studied the etchings of Claude. In asking this, he wrote a sentence of delicate appreciation which I thought it would be well to disseminate and preserve, and so begged permission to quote it. 'His execution,' said Samuel Palmer, 'is of that highest kind which has no independent essence, but lingers and hesitates with the thought, and is lost and found in a bewilderment of intricate beauty.' In this sentence we have the key to the writer's own ways of work as an etcher : he dislikes execution, however brilliant, which is not subordinate to the thought, or, perhaps, to put it more accurately, the best execution, in his view, is tentative, and submissively waits whilst the mind seeks, always humbly following and endeavouring to obey, never hurrying the executive processes till they get ahead of the perceptive and inventive processes. And I venture to add that the beautiful sentence in which Samuel Palmer described the excellence of Claude, is accurately descriptive of his own excellence, and I would have said of Samuel Palmer, if I had known how to write anything so good, just these words, 'His execution is of that highest kind which has no independent essence, but lingers and hesitates with the thought and is lost and found in a bewilderment of intricate beauty.'

And yet I have said that Samuel Palmer's work was false etching, and can false etching be execution of the highest kind? The habit of writing quite sincerely lands us, it appears, in embarrassing contradictions. This artist's method is entirely honest ; it is the method which best interprets his ideas, and so it is execution morally and poetically for him of the highest kind. But there have been aqua-fortists whose execution was equally sincere, equally lingering and hesitating with the thought, and yet true etching in the strictest technical sense. The difference is, that Samuel Palmer is less a true etcher than a noble painter expressing himself with the etching-needle, and however marvellous is the work which he has done on copper, I am inclined to believe that the kind of engraving which would suit his genius best is not etching, but mezzo-tint. Nevertheless, I rejoice that Samuel Palmer has done these etchings, because they prove the versatility and adapt-ability of the art. He has abandoned the strongest point of etching, the vivacity and freedom of the etched line, and he has relied upon qualities which the vulgar do not suppose etching to possess, and which even the most informed judges know to be difficult of attainment by its processes. He has not sought the freedom and keen accent which the method suggests, but has compelled it to give what his own artistic feeling most desired, namely, a most luxuriant indecision, a powerful and elaborate tonality. His plates are not true etchings, relatively to the art, because

[1] 'The Early Ploughman'.

they do not insist upon its especial and peculiar qualities; but they are indeed true relatively to the artist, for they express his profoundest love.[1]

'False etching', in its purely technical aspect, is to be seen in the work of many later etchers, especially in that of Ernest D. Roth whose plates of views in Italy and Turkey were popular at the beginning of the present century. 'We may class him,' wrote Frank Jewett Mather, '. . . with such patient contrivers of full effects as Samuel Palmer . . . ,' and he went on to describe a plate of the Ponte Vecchio, Florence, as being, 'not in the ordinary sense drawn, but fully painted with the needle and the acid.'[2] This, bearing Hamerton's remarks in mind, is pure Palmer.

But there was more than technical achievement in Palmer's etchings, and their most profound influence comes from their visionary content which, in Palmer's own words, 'lingers and hesitates with the thought, and is lost and found in a bewilderment of intricate beauty.' And, he might have added, it lingers and hesitates in the poetry of the earth, the mystic sacramental quality which makes us sense its innate prophecy and fulfilment in the year's death in winter, its resurrection in spring, its fulfilment in summer and autumn. It lingers, too, in the pastoral essence in the nature of the truly innocent man, in his toil and its fruits.

In this sense Palmer's influence is to be seen in particular in the early etchings of Graham Sutherland and in those of Sutherland's contemporary Paul Drury.[3] In these appear even the details loved by Palmer: sheep, shepherd-like figures, primitive cottages, sunrays, trees that express the power of growth, and much more. Sutherland's etchings contained the seeds of much in his later paintings, in which the minutiae of natural forms are magnified so that they are lifted away from their familiar aspect and translated in a manner so unfamiliar as to shock the observer into appreciating previously unsuspected powers in them.

In Sutherland's etching 'Pecken Wood' (1926; Plate 37), there are many elements reminiscent of Palmer. The sunrays at the right-hand side, the painterly tonal quality of the work, deeply-etched lines, the wisps of cirrus clouds in the sky, are all paralleled, as we have seen, in Palmer's etchings. Above all there is that effect mentioned by Palmer in a letter written to T. O. Barlow on 30 September 1876: '. . . those thousand little luminous eyes which peer through a finished linear etching, and in those of Claude are moving sunshine upon dew, or dew upon violets in the shade.'[4]

In Drury's etching 'September' (1928; Plate 38), is expressed some of the lush richness shown by Palmer in 'The Vine' and 'The Morning of Life' (Plates 5 and 10). The laden apple tree and the women with baskets picking up fallen fruit, the sheep, the nearby oast houses (for the scene is set in Palmer's Kent), indicate rich abundance. There are, too, Palmer's favourite glint of water in the

[1] *Etching and Etchers*, pp. 142–4. [2] *The Print Collector's Quarterly*, Vol. I, p. 448 (1911).
[3] *The Print Collector's Quarterly*, Vol. XVI, pp. 76–85 (1929). [4] *Life and Letters*, p. 366.

pond by the cottage, a sky with strato-cumulus clouds, and again something of those 'thousand little luminous eyes', though there are less of them here than in the Sutherland work.

Palmer's etchings have indeed strong parallels in the work of these two etchers. In another way Palmer's influence is present in the etchings of one of the greatest masters of the art – F. L. Griggs.[1] In these are the 'thousand eyes', accurately observed skies with identifiable clouds, sheep, shepherds, moons, rustic chapels, the glint of water, but above all a Gothic spirit, especially in such fantasies as 'Anglia Perdita', 'The Minster' and 'The Barbican'. On the surface these are not strikingly reminiscent of Palmer – not so much, for example, as Griggs's poetic plate of Stoke Poges churchyard – yet his influence is there none the less. It is known that Griggs made a deep study of Palmer's work,[2] and that Palmer saw himself as a 'pure quaint crinkle-crankle Goth'.[3] The Gothic spirit was in fact never far from Palmer : 'These leaves were a Gothic window',[4] he wrote in his sketchbook, seeing, as many others have done, Gothic tracery in foliage. In certain of his etchings this idea seemed to be reflected – especially those in which cypresses inspired by those at the Villa d'Este form part of the composition and suggest the aspiring lines of Gothic architecture. This idea is also evident in Griggs's plate 'Owlpen Manor' (Plate 39).

To go outside the world of etching, Palmer's influence is present in the engraved glasses of Laurence Whistler. Here again are sunrays, primitive cottages, ideal landscapes, skies with identifiable clouds – a rare enough phenomenon in ordinary painting, to say nothing of the difficult medium of engraved glass – moons, stars and trees expressive of the power of growth. But most of all it is the mystical element in Whistler's glasses, that sacramental quality that we have just noted, that relate them to Palmer.[5]

It is a quality which is found also in much poetry, although it would be rash to attribute all of such poetry to Palmer's influence. There are, however, definite links with Palmer in the work of W. B. Yeats, who specifically mentions the artist in one or two of his poems. In 'The Phases of the Moon' for instance :

> We are on the bridge ; that shadow is the tower,
> And the light proves that he is reading still.
> He has found, after the manner of his kind,
> Mere images ; chosen this place to live in

[1] Comstock, Francis Adams, *A Gothic Vision : F. L. Griggs and his work*, Oxford, 1966.

[2] Comstock, *op. cit.* p. 7.

[3] Grigson, *op. cit.* p. 124. The word was not first used by Palmer in connexion with Gothic. John Evelyn spoke of church architecture as consisting largely of 'Sharp angles . . . narrow lights, lame statues, lace and other cut-work and crinkle-crankle'. Williams-Ellis, Clough, *The Pleasures of Architecture* (1954) p. 40.

[4] 1824 Sketchbook, p. 5.   [5] Lister, Raymond, *Great Works of Craftsmanship* (1967) pp. 179–89.

29. William Blake. Wood engraving No. V
from *The Pastorals of Virgil . . . . for Schools*
$1\frac{3}{8} \times 2\frac{15}{16}$ inches
Mrs. Raymond Lister

30. William Blake. Wood engraving No.
XVII from *The Pastorals of Virgil . . . for
Schools*
$1\frac{3}{8} \times 3$ inches
Mrs. Raymond Lister

31. Edward Calvert. The Cyder Feast
Wood engraving. 3 × 5 inches
Mrs. Raymond Lister

32. Edward Calvert. The Brook
Wood engraving. 2 × $3\frac{15}{32}$ inches
Mrs. Raymond Lister

33. Endymion the Shepherd Boy asleep on Mt. Latmos
Sculpture, Graeco-Roman
Trustees of the British Museum

34. Cornfield by Moonlight and Evening Star
Water-colour, gouache and pen. $7\frac{3}{4} \times 11\frac{3}{4}$ inches
Collection of Sir Kenneth Clark

35. The Shearers
Oil and tempera. $20\frac{1}{4} \times 28$ inches
Private collection

36. William Blake. Jacob's Ladder
Water-colour. $14\frac{5}{8} \times 11\frac{1}{2}$ inches
Trustees of the British Museum

37. Graham Sutherland. Pecken Wood
Etching. $5\frac{1}{4} \times 7\frac{1}{4}$ inches
Mrs. Raymond Lister

38. Paul Drury. September
Etching. $3\frac{15}{16} \times 5$ inches
Mrs. Raymond Lister

39. F. L. Griggs. Owlpen Manor
Etching. $7\frac{7}{16} \times 9\frac{5}{16}$ inches
Mrs. Raymond Lister

Because, it may be, of the candle-light
From the far tower where Milton's Platonist
Sat late, or Shelley's visionary prince :
The lonely light that Samuel Palmer engraved,
An image of mysterious wisdom won by toil ;
And now he seeks in book or manuscript
What he shall never find.[1]

As Mr. T. R. Henn has pointed out,[2] many of Palmer's pictures contain this lonely light. But he feels sure, and I agree with him, that Yeats is here referring to the etching 'The Lonely Tower'. Yeats possessed a collection of lantern slides of works by Blake, Calvert and Palmer, and this etching was one of the subjects.[3] And he writes of 'The lonely light that Samuel Palmer *engraved*'. The above lines from 'The Phases of the Moon' were first published in the collection of poems *The Wild Swans at Coole* in 1919. Nearly twenty years later, in 1938, near the end of his life, Yeats was still thinking of Palmer when he wrote his great poem 'Under Ben Bulben' :

When that greater dream had gone
Calvert and Wilson, Blake and Claude,
Prepared a rest for the people of God,
Palmer's phrase, but after that
Confusion fell upon our thought.[4]

Where in this passage he mentions 'Palmer's phrase' Yeats is referring to Palmer's description of Blake's *Virgil* wood engravings which has already been quoted on page 23 : 'They are like all that wonderful artist's works the drawing aside of the fleshly curtain, and the glimpse which all the most holy, studious saints and sages have enjoyed, of that rest which remaineth to the people of God.'[5] But Yeats was wrong to call it 'Palmer's phrase', for St. Paul's Epistle to the Hebrews (IV. 9) contains the words : 'There remaineth therefore a rest to the people of God.'[6]

We have seen that the title of the piece in which Yeats writes of Palmer's 'Lonely light' is 'The Phases of the Moon', and this may serve to remind us of the frequent use of moon symbolism in Palmer's etched and painted work and in Yeats's poetry. In each it symbolises the feminine principle, the soft nocturnal moonlight of Diana, as contrasted with the hard, masculine Apollo-like diurnal

[1] *The Collected Poems of W. B. Yeats* (London, 1961) p. 184.   [2] *The Lonely Tower* (London, 1965, 2nd ed.) p. 254.
[3] Henn, *op. cit.* p. 254.   [4] *Collected Poems*, p. 400.
[5] *Life and Letters*, p. 16.   [6] I am indebted to Dr. Oliver Edwards for drawing my attention to this.

sunlight. In a recently-issued concordance to Yeats's poems,[1] nearly three closely-printed pages are devoted to references to the moon and moonlight. And Palmer's work is full of moons ; his surviving sketchbook contains no less than thirty-three. We have seen how frequently also the moon is depicted in the etchings.

Here and there in Yeats's poetry is a phrase, a sentence or a whole verse that seems to be illuminated by Palmer, though his name may not be mentioned. In this passage, for instance, from 'Love's Loneliness' :

> The mountain throws a shadow,
> Thin is the moon's horn ;
> What did we remember
> Under the ragged thorn ?
> Dread has followed longing,
> And our hearts are torn.[2]

Finally, let us look at one of the etchings left unfinished by Palmer on his death and completed by his son, 'The Homeward Star'. It will be recalled that I consider this to be nearer in spirit to Palmer than any of the other plates completed by A. H. Palmer. It certainly forms a remarkable parallel with Yeats's early and most famous poem. It is, like that work, a vision of the delights of the simple life, the true lyricism of the soil and of those who toil on it.

> I will arise and go now, and go to Innisfree,
> And a small cabin build there, of clay and wattles made :
> Nine bean-rows will I have there, a hive for the honey-bee,
> And live alone in the bee-loud glade.
>
> And I shall have some peace there, for peace comes dropping slow,
> Dropping from the veils of the morning to where the cricket sings ;
> There midnight's all a glimmer, and noon a purple glow,
> And evening full of the linnet's wings.
>
> I will arise and go now, for always night and day
> I hear lake water lapping with low sounds by the shore ;
> While I stand on the roadway, or on the pavements grey,
> I hear it in the deep heart's core.[3]

[1] Parrish, S. M. and Painter, J. A., *A Concordance to the poems of W. B. Yeats* (New York, 1963).

[2] *Collected Poems*, pp. 298–9.

[3] *Complete Poems*. p. 44. See also Lister, Raymond, *Beulah to Byzantium : a study of parallels in the Works of W. B. Yeats, William Blake, Samuel Palmer and Edward Calvert* (Dublin, 1965).

V

A Catalogue
of Samuel Palmer's Etchings

In the following list the terms *left* and *right*, unless otherwise qualified, refer to the viewer's left and right.

Some of the states are difficult to differentiate without having specimens of other states with which to compare them. It should also be remembered that the character of an etching may be considerably altered during printing and therefore some of the points mentioned may be less evident in some impressions than in others. The numbering is intended to supersede that in Alexander's Catalogue (see Bibliography), which was compiled before several of the states described were known. The main public collections of Palmer's etchings are in the British Museum and the Ashmolean Museum. A large number of the states mentioned here exist only in private collections.

1 THE WILLOW (Plate 1) 1850

(i) Plate: $4\frac{5}{8} \times 3\frac{3}{16}$ inches. Etched surface: $3\frac{17}{32} \times 2\frac{5}{8}$ inches. The marginal line is broken at the top corners, bottom left-hand corner and in several places on the left-hand vertical frame line. Just over $\frac{1}{4}$ inch down from the top frame line two of the horizontal sky lines are drawn more widely apart than the others, giving the effect of a leftward extension to the third (from the top) horizontal bar of cloud. There are a number of breaks in the sky lines. Signed in the lower left-hand corner: S. PALMER 1850.

(ii) The breaks in the marginal lines and some of those in the sky lines are repaired. A horizontal line is now drawn between the two sky lines which in state (i) were drawn widely apart. This gives that area of the sky a more regular appearance.

As published in *The Life and Letters of Samuel Palmer* by A. H. Palmer (1892).

(iii) With a small engraved triangle below the lower left-hand corner of the frame line. Each impression is initialled in pencil: F. S., M. H., F. L. G.[1] Printed in 1926.

[1] The initials are those of Sir Frank Short, Martin Hardie and F. L. Griggs.

Impression from cancelled plate.

As state (iii), but without the pencilled initials, and defaced by a vertical line engraved through the centre of the plate.

2 THE SKYLARK (Plate 2) 1850 Steel plate

(i) Plate: $4\frac{7}{8} \times 4\frac{9}{16}$ inches. Etched surface: $3\frac{7}{8} \times 2\frac{7}{8}$ inches. There are no trees beside the cottage on the left. The man and the dog do not cast shadows.

(ii) The man and the dog cast shadows. The trees on the hill and in front of it are more clearly highlighted.

(iii) A branch is added to the left of the tree on the right-hand side about $1\frac{5}{8}$ inches from the top frame line. The size of the lark is increased. Smoke comes from the cottage chimney.

Further work to the sky and clouds.

(iv) The size of the etched surface is increased to $3\frac{7}{8}$ inches in height by a strip of new work in the foreground. Two trees are added between the cottage and the man, above the garden gate. The light on the cornfield now extends to the tree trunks on the right. Three groups of light rays ascend from the centre of the horizon towards the dark cloud. Still further work to the sky and clouds.

Etched signature in left foreground: *S. Palmer.*

(v) The trees at the left near to the cottage have increased foliage above the chimney and new branches on the top right. The sunrays, now brighter, are made into two groups.

(vi) The branch of the tree on the right which was added in state (iii) is extended farther towards the centre.

(vii) The plate is cut down to $4\frac{5}{8} \times 3\frac{13}{16}$ inches. Lettered: *Samuel Palmer. 17.* Published as Plate 17 in *Etchings of the Art Union of London by the Etching Club* (1857).

(viii) As state (vii), but with the light increased on the cornfield and to the front of the dog.

3 THE HERDSMAN'S COTTAGE or SUNSET (Plate 3) 1850 Steel plate

(i) Plate: $4\frac{7}{8} \times 4\frac{5}{8}$ inches. Etched surface: $3\frac{13}{16} \times 3$ inches.

(ii) The width of the plate is reduced to 4 inches. Palmer's initials, s p, are etched in the lower margin below the left-hand corner.

Published in *The Portfolio*, November 1872 (title erroneously given as 'Sunrise'); *Examples of Modern Etching* by P. G. Hamerton (1875); *Etching and Etchers* by P. G. Hamerton (1880, third edition; erroneous title noted). An early trial proof is in the Ashmolean Museum.

4 CHRISTMAS or FOLDING THE LAST SHEEP   (Plate 4)   1850
(i) Plate : $4\frac{7}{8} \times 4\frac{5}{8}$ inches. Etched surface : $3\frac{7}{8} \times 3\frac{3}{16}$ inches.
Most of the lines are weak, the result of unequal biting. The following lines
are strong : Lower boughs of the tree at the left across the roof of the cottage ;
top of the tree at the right ; shepherd's hat ; dog. The signature in the plate
at the bottom right-hand corner is indistinct.
(ii) The unequal biting is largely remedied. The tones and lighting are nearly
completed. The signature is etched plainly.
(iii) The width of the plate is reduced to 4 inches. Some of the lines are
strengthened with a graver.
(iv) As state (iii) but lettered in the centre of the lower margin : *'Christmas'|
From Bampfylde's Sonnet.* ; and in the lower margin below the left-hand
corner : S. Palmer.
Published in *Samuel Palmer A Memoir* by A. H. Palmer (1882).
(v) As states (iii) and (iv) but with the marginal inscription erased. With a
small engraved triangle below the left lower corner of the border line. Each
impression is initialled in pencil : F.S., M.H., F.L.G.[1] Printed in 1926.
Impression from cancelled plate.
As state (v), but without the pencilled initials, and defaced by a vertical line
engraved through the centre of the plate.

5 THE VINE or PLUMPY BACCHUS   (Plate 5)   1852   Plate with two
subjects
(i) Plate : $11\frac{7}{8} \times 8\frac{1}{2}$ inches. Etched surfaces. Upper subject : $3\frac{1}{2} \times 5$ inches.
Lower subject : $2\frac{1}{4} \times 5$ inches. The lower subject is bordered by an etched line.
(ii) As state (i), but the etched border line has been removed from the lower
subject which is vignetted and now measures $2\frac{3}{8} \times 5$ inches.[2]
(iii) The foreground shadows in both subjects are much strengthened giving
greater effect to the figures and to the planes of the compositions. The oval
shape of the bottom subject is more regular.
(iv) Additional work by dry-point has been carried out on the upper subject.
Burrs from this are present on early proofs. The shadow below the right leg of
the kneeling figure extends to the bottom frame line. There is additional
work on the centre of the foreground on the lower subject. This state is
lettered as follows. *Above the upper subject* : THE VINE./SONG IN ANTHONY
AND CLEOPATRA — ACT 2. SCENE 7. *Between the upper and lower subjects* :

[1] See f.n. 1, p. 99.
[2] The British Museum has separate proofs of each subject in this state.

SAMUEL PALMER
COME THOU MONARCH OF THE VINE,
PLUMPY BACCHUS, WITH PINK EYNE:
IN THY VATS OUR CARES BE DROWN'D;
WITH THY GRAPES OUR HAIRS BE CROWN'D;
CUP US, TILL THE WORLD GO ROUND;
CUP US, TILL THE WORLD GO ROUND!

Beneath the lower subject: SAMUEL PALMER

As published in *Songs and Ballads of Shakespeare Illustrated by the Etching Club*, 1853. There were two issues of this publication. The small-paper issue measures $12\frac{5}{8} \times 9\frac{1}{2}$ inches; it is bound in gold-blocked pink cloth. The large-paper issue measures $16\frac{3}{16} \times 10\frac{3}{4}$ inches; it is bound in gold-tooled red morocco and has a different title-page from that of the other issue. The etchings in each issue are alike, except that in the small-paper issue the lettering is printed in black, except for that which appears between the two subjects, which is printed in terra-cotta. In the large-paper issue the lettering above the upper subject and the verse is printed in terra-cotta. The impressions in the large-paper issue are usually more carefully printed than the others.

6 THE SLEEPING SHEPHERD; EARLY MORNING (Plate 6) 1857

Steel plate

(i) Plate: $4\frac{7}{8} \times 4\frac{5}{8}$ inches. Etched surface: $3\frac{3}{4} \times 3\frac{1}{16}$ inches.

The ploughman and oxen are dark against the sky and cast light shadow on the hillside. There is a light spot on the shepherd's right foot about $\frac{1}{32}$ inch diameter. In 1927 the Cotswold Gallery, London, had an impression of this state, inscribed by Palmer: 'Peace and Quiet.' This impression was selected by Palmer to represent his etching at The Art Treasures Exhibition at Manchester in 1857.

(ii) The ploughman, oxen, hill-top and the top of the tree are much lighter. The light on the shepherd's foot has been removed.

(iii) As state (ii), but the width of the plate is reduced to $4\frac{1}{16}$ inches.

(iv) As state (iii) but lettered in the lower margin. *Below the left-hand corner: Samuel Palmer. Below the centre: 5.*

Published as Plate 5 in *Etchings for the Art Union of London by the Etching Club*, 1857.

7 THE RISING MOON or AN ENGLISH PASTORAL (Plate 7) 1857

(i) Plate: $7\frac{1}{16} \times 9\frac{15}{16}$ inches. Etched surface: $4\frac{19}{32} \times 7\frac{1}{2}$ inches. The church tower has a belfry window on the side nearest to the moon; there are also suggestions of a stair turret. The spire on the tower is extended beyond the edge of the hill to the sky. The lines around the moon are broken. The pool on the left extends from the margin of the composition to the house.

(ii) The church spire is shortened; it does not reach the edge of the hill above it. The side of the tower nearest to the moon is cut down to under half its previous width. The belfry window and stair-turret top have disappeared. The pool does not extend to the house, about one third of its length being hidden by the bank.

(iii) The sheep and provender trough in the right foreground cast definite and stronger shadows. That of the latter is like a letter Y on its side, and extends from the trough to the margin. Most of the sheep are altered; the one in the middle is completely remodelled. The thin wisp of horizontal dark drifting clouds reaches from the top of the hill to the zenith over the moon. Two streaks of dark cloud descend in the opposite direction on the other side, above the cypresses.

(iv) The width of the cloud-drift from the hill top is increased. The apex which it forms with the opposite cloud-drift has now moved farther to the right.

(v) The hillside beyond the tower is darkened, showing the tower in grey relief. The two trees to the right of the tallest cypress are joined. The light patch in the landscape to the left of the tower is now incorporated in the tree beneath. The clouds are altered, the general resulting effect being a softening of tone. The foreground shadows are deepened. There are new shadows close to the shepherd and behind the sheep nearest to him.

(vi) The sky at the left is more broken than in state (v). Two diagonal streaks of cloud to the right of the moon are accented by this, and so is a lower group of clouds above the cypresses. The hills are individually more prominently defined. There is halation from the moon's light over the right-hand slope of the hills. The width of the largest window light is reduced. Palmer's initials, s p, are now etched in the lower right-hand corner.

(vii) The size of the plate is reduced to $5\frac{3}{4} \times 8\frac{3}{4}$ inches. The cloud to the right of the moon no longer crosses it, though in some impressions indefinite traces remain. The work on the ground in front of the centre trees is patchy. The fine lines on the buildings are now somewhat worn and uneven. Lettered in the lower margin. *Below the left-hand corner: Samuel Palmer. Below the centre: 10.*

Published as Plate 10 in *Etchings for the Art Union of London by the Etching Club,* 1857.

(viii) As state (vii). Two lighted passages have disappeared, one in the trees just above the head of the second sheep from the right, the other between the sheep and the centre gable of the three-gabled house.

(ix) The trees in the distance between the towers are remodelled and their outline is more sharply defined. The spot of light previously present on the left-hand battlement of the tower has disappeared. The shadow between the cypresses and sheep is darkened.

8 THE WEARY PLOUGHMAN or THE HERDSMAN or TARDUS BUBULCUS (Plate 8) Begun 1858

(i) Plate: $7\frac{1}{2} \times 10\frac{1}{4}$ inches. Etched surface: $5\frac{3}{16} \times 7\frac{15}{16}$ inches. Preliminary state. There are large white patches in the sky, particularly in the centre and right-hand areas. The circle of the moon is complete. There is faulty drawing on the foreleg of the nearer ox.[1]

(ii) The sky as in state (i). The circle of the moon is broken where it touches the mountain. The faulty drawing on the ox is corrected. The smoke from the chimneys is straight and broad.

(iii) The moon is enlarged, but there are traces of its earlier outline on its right side. The farther window-light in the cottage has disappeared. The smoke from the chimney is wavery. More work has been added to the sky which is now almost complete.

(iv) The earlier outline is removed from the right side of the moon. There is a bow of light in the lower sky at the left, reaching from the chestnut tree to the highest rock on the centre of the hill. The background behind the head of the nearer ox is darkened, throwing it into stronger relief. More work has again been added to the sky, especially near to the moon, softening the effect.

(v) A white space about a quarter of an inch above the moon and resembling a script D, which appears in earlier states, now has its upper part shaded over. Above it a curling wisp is now obscured by vertical lines of shading, drawn in the direction of the star nearest the centre. There are two faint lines from the cloud on the left across the edge of the moon.

(vi) The sky has been burnished giving it a more even appearance, except for the area to the right of the moon.

(vii) The faint lines across the face of the moon are extended, reducing the area of its face. A streak of illuminated cloud which appears in previous states above the rocks on the hill is darkened.

(viii) As state (vii) but with the numeral 4 engraved in the centre of the lower margin.

Published in *A Selection of Etchings by the Etching Club*, 1865. Altogether twelve etchings were published in this selection.

---

[1] P. and D. Colnaghi and Co. Ltd. once had in their possession an impression of either state i or ii marked 'Ist. proving July 3, 1858 No. 6'.

9 THE EARLY PLOUGHMAN or THE MORNING SPREAD UPON THE MOUNTAINS (Plate 9)[1] Begun before 1861

(i) Plate: $7 \times 9\frac{7}{8}$ inches. Etched surface: $5\frac{1}{8}$ to $5\frac{3}{16} \times 7\frac{3}{4}$ inches. The ploughman has no hat. The bridge and the tree at the left are not yet etched. The subject is throughout very lightly etched.

(ii) The ploughman's hat is partially drawn. There are traces of an early figure near his. The horns of the nearer oxen are not yet drawn. The bridge and the tree at the left are indistinctly drawn. The forms of the distant hills are indistinct against the sky. There are no light edges to the upper clouds.

(iii) The ploughman's hat is complete. The horns of the oxen are drawn. The bridge and the tree at the left are more distinct. The under-edges of the upper clouds have some light. This has the effect of throwing up the forms of the distant hills in greater relief.

(iv) The height of the tree between the two cypresses on the right and immediately above the woman's figure is increased to within $\frac{13}{16}$ inch of the top of the etching. The ploughman has a patch of white on the right side of his head, appearing as if he is turning to look at the woman.
The tail of the right-hand ox reaches nearly to the flank of the centre ox. The modelling of the oxen is incomplete. The modelling of the tree at the left is incomplete. There is no reflected light under the left-hand arch of the bridge. The parapets of the bridge are distinct.

(v) The top of the third cypress from the left is now sharply pointed instead of rounded. The main ploughing team is more firmly drawn and the horns of the oxen are sharper. The patch of white on the ploughman's head is now shaded. The tail of the right-hand ox is shortened. The forequarters of the nearer ox are now in their final form. More uprising rays of light have been added to the clouds. The reflected light under the centre arch of the bridge is brighter. There is now some light under the left-hand arch of the bridge.

(vi) Generally as state (v) but intensified by rebiting. Two horizontal bars of dark cloud have been added behind the distant crags.

(vii) There is more contrast between the light and dark portions of the sky. The vertical curved wisps of lighted cloud beginning $\frac{3}{8}$ inch to the right of the tower are more emphasised than in earlier states. The cypresses are darker, especially the first three on the left. The tree at the left is more firmly drawn. There is more contrast in the foreground. There are many other minor differences.

(viii) The horizontal streaks of cloud have been removed from behind the distant crags. The contrast between the light and dark clouds has been softened, so that the effect of the lighted clouds has been lessened.

[1] There is in the British Museum a monotype of a subject closely related to this. It is in sepia and shows a mountainous scene with a lake and trees and with a ploughman and his team lightly indicated. It came from the collection of Mrs. John Richmond and is attributed to Palmer.

(ix) As state (viii) but more clearly printed. With a small engraved triangle[1] below the lower left-hand corner of the border line. Each impression is initialled in pencil: F.S., M.H., F.L.G.[2] Printed in 1926.
Impression from cancelled plate.
As state (ix), but without the pencilled initials, and defaced by a vertical line engraved through the centre of the plate.

10 THE MORNING OF LIFE (Plate 10) Begun 1860–1

(i) Plate: $7\frac{1}{8} \times 10$ inches. Etched surface: $5\frac{3}{8} \times 8\frac{1}{4}$ inches. The subject is lightly drawn, the figures sketched. The basket and apples are not drawn. Remains of an earlier subject, 'Hercules and Cacus', may be clearly seen – for example the enlargement of the etched surface is visible.
(ii) The basket of apples is now etched. Three apples lie near it on the grass. The distant landscape between the trees at the left and the centre has taken shape. The figures are nearer to completion.
(iii) The knees of the kneeling woman show clearly between her arms. The head of the figure leaning on the bank, which was originally light, is now dark. The left foreleg of the sheep is not clearly visible.
(iv) On the ground behind the kneeling figure and below the boy pulling on the sheep's horns is a curved twig with three leaves. The outline of the nearest figure has been sharpened with a graver. The nearer hind leg of the sheep is farther back; its earlier position is partly visible.
(v) More work has been done on the nearer hind leg of the sheep, making it more sharply defined.
(vi) The plate is cut down to $5\frac{3}{4} \times 8\frac{1}{2}$ inches. Five apples are clearly drawn. The figures in the foreground are accented. The left shoulder of the nearest sheep-washer is highlighted. The numeral 4 is in the lower left-hand margin.
(vii) The plate is lettered as follows in the lower margin: *Samuel Palmer.* '*The Morning of Life*' 13. The outstretched arm of the left-hand sheep-washer has been highlighted by burnishing. The edge of the left-hand bank of the stream has been similarly burnished. The highlights of the foreground are intensified. Published as Plate 13 in *Etchings for the Art Union of London by the Etching Club*, 1872.

11 THE BELLMAN (Plate 11) Completed 1879

(i) Plate: $7\frac{1}{2} \times 9\frac{7}{8}$ inches. Etched surface: $6\frac{9}{16} \times 9\frac{3}{16}$ inches. The hillside crossing the moon is not yet divided into two planes. The edge of the moon is not yet sharply drawn. There is a diagonal streak of cloud, its under edge

---

[1] Four preliminary proofs without the triangle were made by F. L. Griggs before the edition was printed.
[2] See f.n. 1, p. 99.

brightly lighted, above the first mountain peak from the left of the moon. There is another cloud-streak, in the opposite direction, above the chestnut tree. Reaching from the base of this streak to the top of the chestnut tree is a triangular patch of dark cloud. An inscription is almost burnished away from the lower right-hand corner.

P. and D. Colnaghi and Co. Ltd. once had in their possession the first working proof of this plate. It was touched.

(ii) The moon is outlined but the lines of the sky are not yet extended to it. The streak of cloud over the chestnut tree is darker. The triangular cloud patch below it is now merged into the main forms of the clouds.

According to Alexander *op. cit.* an impression of this state inscribed '3rd proving' is recorded. This, or possibly another similar impression, was once in the possession of P. and D. Colnaghi and Co. Ltd. This bore the date 1st May 1879. It is possible, in view of this, that there was an earlier state than state (i) above.

(iii) The edge of the moon is now sharp. A streak of cloud to its right now extends nearly half way across its face. The cloud above the chestnut is still darker. The tree at the right is darker and more twigs and foliage have been added. One leaf at the left almost touches the disc of the moon. The shadows in the street and on the roof and chimneys at the right have been darkened. New work and an inscription have been added to the lower right-hand corner: S. PALMER. INV. ET. FEC/MEAD. VALE/RED HILL/1879.

(iv) The streak of cloud partly crossing the moon's disc and extending to the right-hand frame line is divided almost throughout its length by a horizontal line, which is double in places. The hillside is clearly divided into two planes where it crosses the face of the moon. The slope of the nearer plane carries two triangular shapes, probably trees, outlined against the moon. There is less light on the chestnut tree. The highlights on the cattle are more accented. There is a general darkening of the composition, especially in the left-hand corner of the foreground and in the street.

(v) A remarque (a branch of a tree) is etched in the lower right-hand margin. Otherwise as state (iv).

Sixty proofs of this state were issued in 1879 by The Fine Art Society.

The Fitzwilliam Museum has an impression of this state printed on vellum.

(vi) The remarque is removed. The plate is lettered as follows in the lower margin: *The Bellman from 'Il Penseroso'. Published by The Fine Art Society,* 148, *New Bond Street, London,* 1879. Otherwise as (iv).

Five impressions of this state were taken on old French paper by F. L. Griggs and each was inscribed by him in pencil.

(vii) The lettering is removed, with a small engraved triangle below the

lower left-hand corner of the border line. Each impression is initialled in pencil: F. S., M. H., F. L. G.[1] Printed in 1926.
Impression from cancelled plate.
As state (vii), but without the pencilled initials, and defaced by a vertical line engraved through the centre of the plate.

12 THE LONELY TOWER   (Plate 12)   Completed 1879
(i) Plate: $7\frac{7}{16} \times 9\frac{15}{16}$ inches. Etched surface: $6\frac{1}{2}$ to $6\frac{9}{16} \times 9\frac{3}{16}$ inches. The subject is in its earliest stages, with slight modelling and lighting. A large leafy bush is lightly etched against a cleft in the rocky bank of the stream. The river in the gorge is light.
(ii) The owl is larger and has white wings. The river is narrower. The large leafy bush has disappeared and its place has been taken by heavy lines. Part of the sky has the appearance of aquatint, probably caused by foul-biting.
(iii) The sky is altered. Three upward wisps of cloud across the moon are replaced by three horizontal bars of light, two across the moon, one above it. The whole composition is darker.
(iv) The foliage on the edge of the chasm in front of the hurdles is darkened so that only its edges are lightened. The sky is lighter above the upper edge of the clump of trees at the right. A signature has now been added to the lower left-hand corner: *Sam.¹ Palmer.*
(v) An extra bar of light has been added to the three previous ones where the moon rises; this is to the right of and just below the first three. The sky is more uniform throughout and lighter still above the trees at the right. The foliage on the hill is more strongly highlighted at its edges. Deeper shadows are cast by the figure and foliage in front of the hurdles.
(vi) As state (v) but with the number 16 added in the lower left-hand margin. Published by R. Ansdell for the Etching Club in *Il Penseroso* 1880.
States (v) and (vi) are usually badly printed.

13 OPENING THE FOLD or EARLY MORNING   (Plate 13)   1880
(i) Plate: $6\frac{7}{16} \times 9\frac{1}{16}$ inches. Etched surface: $4\frac{5}{8} \times 6\frac{15}{16}$ inches. The subject is incomplete. There are no dotted cloud lines between the hills. The sunrays from the horizon do not join those of the upper sky. The head of the figure opening the fold is upright. There are white spaces where the distant figures at the left will later be drawn. A sprig and leaf of the nearest tree are not yet in relief against the light part of the sky.
(ii) The subject is completed. Dotted lines have been added to the sky

¹ See f.n. 1, p. 99.

between the hills. The sunrays are continuous from the horizon to the upper sky. The head of the figure opening the fold is inclined over his right shoulder. The figures at the left are drawn. The sprig and leaf of the nearest tree are now in full relief against the light part of the sky. There is a remarque (a spray of harebells) in the lower margin at the left.

(iii) As state (ii) but with a signature added in the lower left-hand corner: S. PALMER INV & FEC.

(iv) As state (iii) but with a publication line added: *Published by the Fine Art Society*, 148, *New Bond Street, London, W.* 1880.

(v) As state (iv) but with the remarque removed.

(vi) As state (v) but with the publication line removed.

(vii) As state (vi) but the size of the plate is reduced to $5\frac{15}{16} \times 8\frac{7}{16}$ inches. As published in the first (large paper) edition of *An English Version of the Eclogues of Virgil* by Samuel Palmer, 1883.

(viii) As state (vii) but with a verse added in the lower margin:

> *And folded flocks were loose to browse anew*
> *O'er mountain thyme or trefoil wet with dew.*

As published in the second (small paper) edition of *An English Version of the Eclogues of Virgil* by Samuel Palmer, 1884.

(ix) The lettering is removed. Most impressions of this rare state bear the Dover's House Press, Campden, stamp — a monogram consisting of the letters D H P, with the D in reverse, and the cross-bar of the H supporting a cross.

(x) With a small engraved triangle below the lower left-hand corner of the border line. Each impression is initialled in pencil: F. S., F. L. G., M. H.[1] Printed in 1926.

Impression from cancelled plate.

As state (x) but without the pencilled initials, and defaced by a vertical line engraved through the centre of the plate.

[1] See f.n. 1, p.99.

VI

Etchings Begun by Samuel Palmer and Completed by A. H. Palmer

14 THE HOMEWARD STAR   (Plate 14)   Published 1883, 1884
(i) Plate: $5\frac{1}{4} \times 7\frac{3}{8}$ inches. Etched surface: $3\frac{15}{16} \times 5\frac{15}{16}$ inches. Without lettering.
As published in the first (large paper) edition of *An English Version of the Eclogues of Virgil* by Samuel Palmer, 1883.
(ii) As state (i), but with verse added in the lower margin:

> *See, glimmering in the West, the homeward star;*
> *And from the crest of upland towns afar*
> *The hearth-smoke rise; —*

As published in the second (small paper) edition of *An English Version of the Eclogues of Virgil* by Samuel Palmer, 1884.
(iii) The lettering is removed. Only twenty impressions were taken. Each bears the Dover's House Press stamp.[1] Printed in 1924.
(iv) With a small engraved triangle below the lower left-hand corner of the border line.

15 THE CYPRESS GROVE   (Plate 15)   Published 1883, 1884
Plate: $5\frac{3}{16} \times 7\frac{3}{8}$ inches. Etched surface: $3\frac{15}{16} \times 5\frac{15}{16}$ inches. Without lettering. Signed in the lower left-hand corner: s. PALMER.
As published in the first (large paper) edition of *An English Version of the Eclogues of Virgil* by Samuel Palmer, 1883.
(ii) With verse added in the lower margin:

> *Untimely lost, and by a cruel death,*
> *The Nymphs their Daphne's mourn'd with falt'ring breath.*

As published in the second (small paper) edition of *An English Version of the Eclogues of Virgil* by Samuel Palmer, 1884.

[1] See p. 109.

(iii) The lettering is removed. Only eight impressions were taken. Each bears the Dover's House Press stamp.[1] Printed in 1924.

(iv) With a small engraved triangle below the lower left-hand corner of the border line.

16 THE SEPULCHRE   (Plate 16)   Published 1883, 1884

(i) Plate: $5\frac{3}{16} \times 7\frac{3}{8}$ inches. Etched surface: $3\frac{15}{16} \times 5\frac{15}{16}$ inches. Without lettering.

As published in the first (large paper) edition of *An English Version of The Eclogues of Virgil* by Samuel Palmer, 1883.

(ii) With verse added in the lower margin:

> *— while the troubled moon shrunk in and set,*
> *Th' earth trembled, and the starless heav'n was jet.*

As published in the second (small paper) edition of *An English Version of the Eclogues of Virgil* by Samuel Palmer, 1884.

(iii) The lettering is removed. The number of impressions taken is not recorded, but there were probably only a few. Each bears the Dover's House Press stamp.[2] Printed in 1924.

(iv) With a small engraved triangle below the lower left-hand corner of the border line.

17 MOERIS AND GALATEA   (Plate 17)   Published 1883, 1884

(i) Plate: $5\frac{3}{16} \times 7\frac{3}{8}$ inches. Etched surface: $3\frac{15}{16} \times 5\frac{15}{16}$ inches. Without lettering.

As published in the first (large paper) edition of *An English Version of the Eclogues of Virgil* by Samuel Palmer, 1883.

(ii) With verse added in the lower margin:

> *The cream-bowl set and in our cave recline,*
> *(Its brows with poplar shaded, watch the West),*
> *And timely, with the sun, together rest.*

As published in the second (small paper) edition of *An English Version of the Eclogues of Virgil* by Samuel Palmer, 1884.

(iii) The lettering is removed. The number of impressions taken is not recorded, but there were probably only a few. Each bears the Dover's Head Press stamp.[3] Printed in 1924.

---

[1] See p. 109.   [2] See p. 109.   [3] See p. 109.

(iv) With a small engraved triangle below the lower left-hand corner of the border line.

Original Copper Plates

Some of the original copper plates for Samuel Palmer's etchings still exist, but several were destroyed. According to a copy of a statement said to have been written by Palmer,[1] the following were destroyed (the numbers are those in the foregoing list): 2, 5, 6, 7, 8, 10, 12. Despite this, the plate for no. 12 still exists; it is owned by Mr. David Gould, to whom I am indebted for the following details.

The cancelled plate for no. 9 is in the Victoria and Albert Museum. The cancelled plates for nos. 14, 15, 16, and 17 are in the British Museum, to which they were presented in March 1959 by Mr. Gould. *The Homeward Star* (14), *The Cypress Grove* (15), and *The Sepulchre* (16) are all stamped on the back: Hughes and Kimber. *Moeris and Galatea* (17) has the initials E H scratched on the back.

The Lonely Tower (12) was cancelled but has been restored by being knocked up from the back. This restoration was carrried out by Macbeth Raeburn, and a proof was taken at the Liverpool School of Art. The plate shows only minor alterations and could thus be printed from again. Apart from a few experimental prints taken from the plate in this latest state, there has been no edition published and it has therefore not been described in my list.

[1] Ivimy MSS.

APPENDIX A

Calculations by Samuel Palmer showing details of his Income and Expenditure[1]

Profits including house

1839	101	–	7	–	6			
1840	171	–	8	–	9			
1841	158	–	15	–	3			
	3)431	–	11	–	6			
	143	–	17	–	2			

Gross income of 1840

£173   Frames   3 – 3 – 0

Income 1841

£150 – 15 – 8

Income, Italy 1839

I	Fordman	30	–	0	–	0		
N	American	13	–	2	–	0		
C	Lodgers, say	10	–	0	–	0		
O	Mr. Martin	5	–	5	–	0		
M		58	–	7	–	6	(sic)	
E	Danieli	20	–	0	–	0		
	M. Angelo							
T	Raffaellis	20	–	0	–	0		
A	Loggia							
X		98	–	7	–	6		

98	–	7	–	6		
25	–	0	–	0	outlay for trade	
73	–	7	–	6		
28	–	0	–	0		
101	–	7	–	6		

[1] Ivimy MSS.

Drawbacks 1839
Travelling expense   20 – 0 – 0
Loss Picture about   10 – 0 – 0
Say in 1839 half   =
                           5 – 0 – 0
Travelling   20 – 0 – 0
                          _____
                          25 – 0 – 0

Trade expenses in 1840 from Jan. 17.

Colors (*sic*)	4 – 7½ [1]	Brought over 7–11– 8½
Priming brush	10	9– 6– 1 Brown
Glue	3½	6 loss of print
Paintg tablet	4 – 0	6–11 Druggett and
Porterage box fol.	1 – 0	King (?)
Frame [2]	11 – 4	16– 0 5 Best
Drawg paper	14 – 2	okers (*sic*)
Hagt (?) Tools	8 – 0	1– 0– 0 [2] 3–15–0
Card boards	9 – 5	6– 0 say extra 1–0–0
Brush	1 – 0	shirt 18/– say 6
Trac. paper	8	1– 2 box
Drawg do.	1 – 6	4– 0 Hat 8
Colors (*sic*)	6 – 6	4–11½ Carpet
Sundries	2 – 2	2–18– 9 Clothes
Art letters (?)	6	4– 0 Cloak
Paper	1 – 0	Davis Fresnoy (?)
do	3 – 0	15– 0 2 – 0 – 0 (?)
Silk handk.ˢ	5 – 0	_____
Trac. paper	3	23– 8– 4 (*sic*)
Travelling	2–14 – 0	4– 4 From little book

7–11 – 8½ (*sic*)   173–19– 1
                          23– 8– 0
                          _____
                          150–17– 1 (*sic*)

24 – 4 – 7¾ Repairs
Say   6 – 0 – 0 Repairs of trade premises
Brought over   23 – 8 – 4
                  _____
                  29 – 8 – 4

[1] This is deleted.   [2] Word illegible.

[114]

	£	s	d	
	173	17	1	
	29	8	4	
	143	8	9	Profit
	28	0	0	House
	171	8	9	

Income 1841 150 – 15 – 8

Trade expenditure

	£	s	d		£	s	d	
Brown	9	6	1 x					
Notepaper trade		1	6					
Sealing wax trade			4					
Envelopes do.			3					
Hog (?) tools		2	0					
Baise & job frames	5	0	0					
Stamp			3					
Brown's bill	5	18	6					
Shell gold		1	4		40	12	11	
Receipt			3		11	12	6	Subsn. (?) and frames
Dorset travel	4	15	5					
Stamp			6		29	0	5	
Bristol board		1	6					
Sundries	1	0	0					
Mount		1	0					
Receipt		1	6		130	15	3	
Arnoi (?) frame		7	6		28	0	0	
Golding		17	0					
Frames	5	8	0		158	15	3	
Not paid 1841								
Brown	6	5	0					
	39	7	11					
	1	5	0	Sundries				
	40	12	11					

Frames

5	–	0	–	0	
		7	–	6	
		17	–	0	
5	–	8	–	0	
11	–	12	–	6	

Income   150   – 15 – 8

Trade exp.   29   – 0 – 5

(*sic*) 130 – 15 – 3   Profit

Income 1842
Trade expense
Brown's expense

Brings pictr. from Gally.	2 –	6
Porterage	(5 –	0
	(3 –	0
In Travelling	12 –	2
Stamp	–	3
Sepia & chalk	1 –	9
Gray boards	5 –	10
Drawg. paper	1 –	1
Clothes 1 – 13 – 0 [¹]	16 –	6
Cleaning watch	3 –	0
Writing paper & env.	3 –	0
Miss Heals (?) lunch	3 –	0

Income

5	–	5	–	0
1	–	2	–	8
10	–	0	–	0
6	–	11	–	0
5	–	5	–	0
		10	–	0 pro (?)
19	–	19	–	0
2	–	8	–	4
51	–	1	–	0

Income of 1842 to
12 July about

Ex.

51	–	1	–	0
4	–	17	–	11½
46	–	3	–	1½ (*sic*)

Net Income

46	–	3	–	1½	
14	–	0	–	0	Half of Gross Rate of House
60	–	3	–	1½	

¹ This is deleted.

[116]

Trade expenses of 1842

Porterage		2	—	6
Deposit kept		5	—	0
P——		3	—	0
Lee		12	—	2
Stamp x		2	—	3
Materi[al]		1	—	9
Boards		5	—	0
Mat [erial]		1	—	1
Mat [erial]	1 —	13	—	0
Mat [erial]		3	—	0
do		2	—	0
do		1	—	0
do		1	—	6
[1]		10	—	0
[1]				6
Lee		6	—	0
Mat [eria]l		6	—	0
do		2	—	$0\frac{1}{2}$
do				8
,,				4

4 — 17 — $11\frac{1}{2}$ (*sic*)

1 Word illegible.

APPENDIX B

Extract from a Letter Written by A. H. Palmer
to Martin Hardie concerning Frederick Goulding[1]

The letter is dated 16 March 1910 and is written from Post Office Box 294, Vancouver City, British Columbia.

To appreciate Goulding and his workmanship fully, one must have met, what I doubt if you ever encountered, an unfavourable specimen of the species of printer who put the etcher on his mettle (or deep in despondency), by disillusioning him with brutal frankness and in every possible way. He was dense, hide-bound, sordid, and sometimes flagrantly dishonest. He had the inflexibility of a crude machine without machinery's susceptibility of adjustment. His absurdly limited knowledge and vocabulary made it useless to appeal to him in terms outside the every-day patter of his trade; and as the 'Painter Etcher' could not translate his own yearnings into cockney workshop jargon, there was a dead-lock to begin with. Some etchers never seemed to learn that as this formidable middle-man stood between the public and themselves, inexorably, it would have been wise to give up seeking for the impossible. But fair the *ignis fatuus* of their ideal lured them away from the easier and more rational but not less fascinating way of working on the unfamiliar surface and of dealing with mordants given to cruel practical jokes.

By degrees, some reform in printing became imperative, and an energetic practical reform appeared in the person of Frederick Goulding. It was significant of the timid way in which the new type of semi-vicarious etching peeped round the wings of the stage where soon afterwards it danced the can-can, that when Goulding's employers began to realise his value they tentatively promoted him and his press from the jungle of other presses to a sort of little loose-box in the most inaccessible possible place. It was one day in 1873 that I stumbled up stairs dark and many, and stood snuffing up the odour so dear and sometimes so terrible to the etcher. Confronting me was a short, alert, and most pleasant-spoken old gentleman who appeared to preside. This was Goulding's father; and as he introduced me to his son, it struck me that their relations were as they should be. The tall delicate-looking, rather bald man who, with a cigarette in his mouth, bent over the heater, looked very different from the type I knew; and as he held out his

[1] Hardie, Martin, *Frederick Goulding*, pp. 120–7.

wrist to be shaken, his first few sentences showed that he was so indeed. It is true that his plain black apron and rolled-up shirt sleeves showed no trace of artistic 'side'; but there was no trace of trade reserve. There was a courteous and genial kindness of manner; and an evident wish to advance my father's object – the setting up of a private press for our own use, and the thorough grounding of myself in technique. With Goulding's phenomenal intelligence, and his profound and eclectic knowledge of printing, it did not take him many minutes to show me the fallacy of what my father had been joyfully imbibing from Mr. Hamerton as to toy presses with baby leverage – that is for the class of work we wished to turn out. From this cul-de-sac Goulding fetched me with surprising swiftness; and I remember my disappointment at finding that I could not that very day carry home the press under my arm. He gave his reasons for all he said, and finally consented to order a small, heavy press with a star affording reasonable leverage. It was here that his grasp of detail and originality first showed itself. He pointed out that, for the best results in printing certain kinds of etchings, the proportions of the rollers of the ordinary press were wrong, and why they were wrong. Also, that the space provided for the cardboard packing was sometimes insufficient, and the result. Also that in the case of this proposed little press, an iron plank was a necessary evil.

In due course the press and the rest of the gear were installed at Furze Hill House. We had asked for a thoroughly sound and detailed grounding in the modern method of printing etchings on various papers, from thick Whatman to Japanese and India; and, of course, my father and I were thoroughly used to judging the merits of his own and other proofs beforehand. Goulding saw to it that I should begin at the very beginning, to describe which I will not attempt. Long ago he had grasped the fact, as some of his predecessors certainly did not, that for certain plates the richest ink was necessary. He had therefore sent down a large stone muller and some very ancient and valuable oil. We took from a lumber closet the same great grinding slab on which at Shoreham, fifty years before, my father had ground his colours, and proceeded to the vital mysteries of mixing. As to the rest – I am a very light weight; the weather was hot, and the knack not easy to catch; so I can still remember what that black paste of exceeding stiffness and smoothness cost me before it was made to Goulding's mind. This was not merely a lesson in ink-making, but in the fastidiousness and patience and thoroughness that go to make a good printer. We soon put aside the two simple plates Goulding had brought down as unnecessary; and got to grips with my father's; that is to say with common-sense, not extravagant 'retroussage'. Here I was able to hold my own; and the proofs we proceeded to pull, turn and turn about, beat any that had been pre-viously produced. I have them still. Entomology, to say nothing of drawing, had taught me something about delicacy of touch; and it was now that I began to realise Goulding's powers in that way. He had all his facts and processes neatly arranged in his mind; and the gift of eliminating from his teaching all that was not essential, to make room for the essential. This he explained in terms so clear and emphatic that there could be no misunderstanding. I found it easy as we went along to write a series of notes on every process. Yet what he taught me was of course the mere fringe of his own vast knowledge.

APPENDIX C

Samuel Palmer's Wood-block Illustrations for Charles Dickens's *Pictures from Italy*[1]

The first drawings executed upon the wood-block by Palmer and intended as book-illustrations were apparently the designs for *Pictures from Italy*; these are four in number, representing the Street of the Tombs, Pompeii; the Villa D'Este at Tivoli, from the Cypress Avenue; the Colosseum of Rome; and a Vineyard Scene. One of the artist's memorandum-books contains an entry recording the receipt from the publishers of twenty guineas for these drawings. Samuel Palmer and Charles Dickens were never on terms of intimacy; however the acquaintance originated has never transpired, nor does the artist's son, Mr. A. H. Palmer, remember his father ever referring to the subject. It is probable that the novelist's attention had been directed to Palmer's excellent rendering of Italian scenery, which had attracted considerable notice among artists, and that, having met him, he found a degree of warm enthusiasm for that scenery which was so unusual, that he felt convinced that the illustrating of the 'Pictures' could not be placed in better hands. Palmer accepted the commission, but, like all his drawings that were destined to be engraved on wood, it somewhat perplexed him, for reasons presently to be explained. A correspondence of a formal business character ensued, and of the few letters still extant I am enabled to print the following, which endorses the belief that an interview had taken place between author and artist.

'DEVONSHIRE TERRACE,
Wednesday, Thirteenth May 1846.

'Dear Sir, – I beg to assure you that I would on no account dream of allowing the book to go to press without the insertion of your name in the title-page. I placed it there myself, two days ago.

'I have not seen the designs, but I have no doubt whatever (remembering your sketches) that they are very good.

Dear Sir, faithfully yours,   CHARLES DICKENS.
'SAMUEL PALMER, Esq.'

Two of the woodcuts, viz., those printed on the first and last pages of the little book, were designed to allow the text to be dropped in. Sketches (or rather finished

1 Kitton, Frederic G., *Dickens and his Illustrators*, London, 1899, pp. 183–8.

drawings) were made on paper before the subjects were copied by the artist upon the wood-blocks, which drawings, by the way, are much inferior to the artist's water-colours of the same or similar subjects. It seems evident, from the word 'On' being tentatively introduced at the top of the original sketch of the Villa D'Este, that this illustration was at first intended to be placed at the beginning of the chapter entitled 'Going through France', instead of appearing (as it eventually did) in conjunction with the opening lines of the preliminary chapter, – 'The Reader's Passport'. It was apparently Palmer's proposal to insert on the block a decorative letter 'S', but Dickens, in a letter to the artist, says, 'I am afraid I cannot comfortably manage an S. What do you say to the word "On"? Could you possibly do that?'

With regard to the treatment of these illustrations, there is no doubt that they are faithful representations of Nature, adapted from sketches made on the spot. As a matter of fact, it was directly contrary to the artist's habit and principles to transcribe a sketch detail for detail. Although the character of his drawing was somewhat involved, rendering more difficult the work of the engraver, the woodcuts (which bear no signature) are most carefully executed. Notwithstanding this, Mr. A. H. Palmer assures me that these designs, and the rendering of them by the wood-engraver, were not of a kind to which the artist could look back with much satisfaction.

Mr. A. H. Palmer still retains in his possession a drawing on wood by his father of the Villa D'Este, the second illustration in 'Pictures from Italy', which was apparently discarded because the artist had omitted to reverse his design, and therefore could not be properly adapted to the particular page for which it was prepared. Those who are familiar with the freedom and vigour of Samuel Palmer's work from Nature will realise at a glance that he was not at his ease upon wood. In the margin of this drawing the artist pencilled the following instructions to the engraver, who had not entirely succeeded in producing the more subtle effects :

'I wish the thin cypress to be very much as it *appears upon the block* – not lighter. Now that the trees have been darkened, it will be necessary to leave the lines of the building *quite* as thick as they are drawn, letting them gradually gain more strength as they come downwards towards the steps. The degree of sharpness with which the drawing terminates toward the letterpress is just what I wish.'

From this and the following notes, minutely written upon the two retouched proofs of the engraving of this subject, we discover how very much too sanguine the artist was as to the result of the translation of his work, the voluminous directions clearly indicating his solicitude respecting the treatment of microscopic details in his design, the alleged importance of which would be quite beyond the comprehension of an ordinary engraver. Palmer subsequently learnt by experience that his drawing on wood was practically untranslatable as he preferred to offer it for engraving.

MS. *Notes on the First Proof*

'(1.) In both proofs the top of the cypress is very indistinct, which greatly injures the design.

'(2.) From A to B the illuminated side of the cypress has lost its tint in both impressions, which is ruinous to the effect, as the eye can no longer follow it as a simple object distinct from the building from the top to the bottom of the design. The top of the building, too, in both impressions, is nearly invisible, as if the inking had failed. It is very important that this should be rectified, so as not to appear in the printing of the work, as otherwise it will spoil the whole work. I have worked upon building and cypress a little in pencil to show how they ought to have come even in a faint impression.

'(3.) Opposite this mark the light on the cypress stems has been carried down a little lower, and two or three fine threads of light have been introduced into the shadowed side (which are intended to be scarcely perceptible) to remove a blottiness in the dark.

'(4.) The touches on the steps, the statue, and the whole of the lower part of the trees and ground, though not very numerous, are very important to the finish of the foreground.

'(5.) The darkest lines in the great vase have been thinned in the *slightest degree*.

'(6.) Close to C the thickness of a black line on the edge of the cypress has been split.

'(7.) From E down to F a minute speck of light has here and there been inserted on the outline of the cypress foliage to split some blots of dark which will be seen on the untouched proofs, and which were rather harsh.

'(8.) The light flashing on the steps ought to make thinner without removing the outline of the arm of the statue. The foot resting upon the pedestal should be indicated. The action of the other leg thrown back is shown in the retouching by the removal of the black line.

'(9.) The getting the upper part of the slender cypress of as full a tint as I have given it here seems to me so important that if it can be done in no other way, I think a piece should be inserted into the block to effect it. In the drawing on the block it was like this, which I have retouched with pencil.'

Second Proof

'(1.) Opposite are a few touches on the slender cypress, — two very thin lines of light on the stem. Specks of light on the foliage.

'(2.) There is a thick black line on the block, thus which I have here crossed with specks of white; although it is in the body of the tree, it kills the fine work on the Villa.

'(3.) The thickness of outline on the light side of this vase unfinishes the foreground. I have altered it.

'(4.) The thick outline on this leaf unfinishes everything about it.'

Thus we discover how fastidious to a degree was the artist in his desire that every subtle touch of his poetic pencil should be reproduced — a result which, as he quickly perceived, it was impossible to achieve.

Samuel Palmer took a still keener delight in Literature than he did in Art. An insatiable but punctilious reader, the novels of Dickens and Scott were among the very few works of fiction which he read aloud to members of his own household. Mr. A. H. Palmer informs me that he has known his father to be so engrossed by reading aloud one of Dickens's finer and more exciting passages, that the announcement and entry of a visitor served to stop the reading only for a few moments ; the crisis past, he laid down the book and apologised. Literature, indeed, constituted the chief pleasure of his simple life — a life that, at one period at least, would have been almost insupportable without the consolation afforded by books. Early in May 1881, he became, alas ! too ill to work, and on the twenty-fourth of that month he passed peacefully away, leaving behind him a reputation which is blameless.

BIBLIOGRAPHY

ALEXANDER, R. G.
A Catalogue of the Etchings of Samuel Palmer, London, 1937. Publication No. 16 of the Print Collectors' Club.

ASHMOLEAN MUSEUM
Paintings and Drawings by Samuel Palmer, Oxford, n.d.

BINYON, LAURENCE
The Followers of William Blake, London, 1925.

[CALVERT, SAMUEL]
A Memoir of Edward Calvert Artist by His Third Son, London, 1893.

[FINCH, MRS. ELIZA]
Memorials of the Late Francis Oliver Finch, London, 1865.

GILCHRIST, ALEXANDER
Life of William Blake, London, 1942. There are several other, earlier, editions.

GRIGSON, GEOFFREY
The Harp of Aeolus, London, 1948.
Samuel Palmer's Valley of Vision, London, 1960
Samuel Palmer the Visionary Years, London, 1947.

HAMERTON, PHILIP GILBERT
Etching and Etchers, London, 1868. Other editions were issued in 1876 and 1880.

HARDIE, MARTIN
'The Etched Work of Samuel Palmer', *Print Collector's Quarterly*, Vol. 3, pp. 207–40. Boston, Mass., 1913.
Frederick Goulding Master Printer of Copper Plates, Stirling, 1910.
Samuel Palmer, London, 1928. Publication No. 7 of the Print Collectors' Club.

LAVER, JAMES
A History of British and American Etching, London, 1929.

LISTER, RAYMOND
Beulah to Byzantium: a Study of Parallels in the Works of W. B. Yeats, William Blake, Samuel Palmer & Edward Calvert, Dublin, 1965.
Edward Calvert, London, 1962.

LISTER, RAYMOND
'Francis Oliver Finch', *Studies in the Arts*, edited by Francis Warner, pp. 99—115. Oxford, 1968.
William Blake. An Introduction to the Man and to his Work, London, 1968.

MALINS, EDWARD
Samuel Palmer's Italian Honeymoon, 1968.

PALMER, A. H.
The Life and Letters of Samuel Palmer Painter and Etcher, London, 1892.
Samuel Palmer a Memoir, London, 1882.

REDGRAVE, F. M.
Richard Redgrave, London, 1891.

ROGET, JOHN LEWIS
A History of the 'Old Water-Colour Society', 2 vols., London, 1891.

STEPHENS, F. G.
Notes by F. G. Stephens on a Collection of Drawings, Paintings and Etchings by the late Samuel Palmer, London, 1881.

STIRLING, A. M. W.
The Richmond Papers, London, 1926.

STORY, ALFRED T.
James Holmes and John Varley, London, 1894.
The Life of John Linnell, 2 vols., London, 1892.

VICTORIA AND ALBERT MUSEUM
Catalogue of an Exhibition of Drawings, Etchings & Woodcuts by Samuel Palmer and other Disciples of William Blake, London, 1926.

WEDMORE, FREDERICK
Etching in England, London, 1895.

Index